SNAPREVISE

UCAT Guide & Getting Into Medicine
2024–2026

Afia Anzum and Timothy Falloon

InStudent Education UK Ltd owner of SnapRevise® trademark.
43 Priston Close, Worle, BS22 7FL, Weston-Super-Mare, United Kingdom

www.snaprevise.co.uk

Copyright © InStudent Publishing Pty Ltd 2024

All rights reserved. These notes are protected by copyright owned by InStudent Publishing Pty Ltd and you may not reproduce, disseminate, or communicate to the public the whole or a substantial part thereof except as permitted at law or with the prior written consent of InStudent Publishing Pty Ltd.

Title: SnapRevise UCAT and Medical Entry Guide
ISBN: 978-1-917424-00-4

Published by InStudent Education UK Ltd CN 15550989 under licence from InStudent Publishing Pty Ltd.
ACN 624 188101

Disclaimer

No reliance on warranty. These SnapRevise materials are intended to supplement but are not intended to replace or to be any substitute for your regular school attendance, for referring to prescribed texts, or for your own note taking. You are responsible for following the appropriate syllabus, attending school classes, and maintaining good study practices. It is your responsibility to evaluate the accuracy of any information, opinions, and advice in these materials. Under no circumstance will InStudent Publishing Pty Ltd or InStudent Education UK Ltd ("Publishers"), their officers, agents, or employees be liable for any loss or damage caused by your use or reliance on these materials, including any adverse impact upon your performance in any academic subject as a result of your use or reliance on the materials. You accept that all information provided or made available by the Publishers is in the nature of general information and does not constitute advice. It is not guaranteed to be error-free and you should always independently verify any information, including through use of a professional teacher and other reliable resources. To the extent permissible at law, the Publishers expressly disclaim all warranties or guarantees of any kind, whether express or implied, including without limitation any warranties concerning the accuracy or content of information provided in these materials or other fitness for purpose. The Publishers shall not be liable for any direct, indirect, special, incidental, consequential or punitive damages of any kind. You agree to indemnify the Publishers, its officers, agents, and employees against any loss whatsoever by using these materials.

Contents

I	**The UCAT**	**1**
1	**Section 1 – Verbal Reasoning**	**3**
	1.1 Introduction	3
	1.2 Core skills	3
	1.2.1 Critical thinking	3
	1.2.2 Logical reasoning	4
	1.2.3 Deductive reasoning	4
	1.2.4 Inductive reasoning	4
	1.2.5 Abductive reasoning	5
	1.2.6 Reading proficiency and speed reading	5
	1.3 General advice for Section 1	6
	1.3.1 How to prepare	6
	1.3.2 Tips for staying on time	7
	1.3.3 Running out of time	8
	1.4 Strategy for *True-False-Can't-Tell* questions	8
	1.4.1 Defining *True*, *False* and *Can't Tell*	9
	1.5 Strategy for Free Text questions	12
	1.5.1 How to approach questions with a specific stem	12
	1.5.2 How to approach questions with a generic stem	14
	1.6 Sample questions	16
	1.7 Answers to sample questions	18
2	**Section 2 – Decision Making**	**19**
	2.1 Introduction	19
	2.2 Core skills	20
	2.2.1 Logical reasoning	20
	2.2.2 Statistical reasoning	25
	2.2.3 Evaluating arguments	26
	2.3 General advice for Section 2	27
	2.3.1 How to prepare	27
	2.3.2 Tips for staying on time	27
	2.3.3 Running out of time	28
	2.4 Strategy for *Yes and No* questions	28
	2.4.1 Skills assessed by this question format	28
	2.4.2 How scoring works	28
	2.5 Strategy for *Single Best Answer* questions	31
	2.5.1 Skills assessed by this question format	31
	2.6 Sample questions	33
	2.7 Answers to sample questions	34
3	**Section 3 – Quantitative Reasoning**	**35**
	3.1 Introduction	35
	3.2 Core skills	35
	3.2.1 Ratios	35
	3.2.2 Percentages	37
	3.2.3 Financial mathematics	38
	3.2.4 Statistics	40
	3.2.5 Physics	41

		3.3 General advice for Section 3	42
		3.3.1 How to prepare	42
		3.3.2 Tips for staying on time	43
		3.3.3 Running out of time	43
	3.4	Strategy for associated questions	44
	3.5	Strategy for standalone questions	46
		3.5.1 Saving time	47
	3.6	Sample questions	49
	3.7	Answers to sample questions	50
4	**Section 4 – Abstract Reasoning**		**51**
	4.1	Introduction	51
	4.2	Core skills	52
		4.2.1 Pattern recognition	52
		4.2.2 Time management	52
	4.3	General advice for Section 4	52
		4.3.1 How to prepare	56
		4.3.2 List of pattern types	57
	4.4	Strategy for type 1: *Set A, B, or Neither* questions	59
	4.5	Strategy for type 2: *Next in the Sequence* questions	61
	4.6	Strategy for type 3: *Complete the Statement* questions	63
	4.7	Strategy for type 4: *Pick Which Set* questions	64
	4.8	Sample questions	67
	4.9	Answers to sample questions	71
5	**Section 5 – Situation Judgement Test**		**74**
	5.1	Introduction	74
	5.2	Core skills	75
		5.2.1 Reading proficiency and speed reading	75
		5.2.2 Empathy and compromise	75
	5.3	General advice for Section 5	75
		5.3.1 Judging appropriateness	76
		5.3.2 Practice log of ethical issues	77
		5.3.3 Medical ethics terminology	79
		5.3.4 Assessing perspectives	80
		5.3.5 Short-term and long-term importance	80
	5.4	Strategy for appropriateness questions	82
	5.5	Strategy for importance questions	82
	5.6	Sample questions	84
	5.7	Answers to sample questions	86
6	**UCAT preparation advice**		**87**
	6.1	Practice questions	87
	6.2	Exam strategies	87
	6.3	Advice for sitting the UCAT	88
II	**Medical interviews**		**90**
1	**Interview advice**		**91**
	1.1	SS panel universities and dates	91
	1.2	MMI universities and dates	92
	1.3	Why choose Medicine	94
	1.4	Interview preparation	95
	1.5	List of potential interview questions	96
	1.6	General interview advice	103
	1.7	Semi-structural panel interview preparation and advice	104
	1.8	MMI preparation and advice	107
	1.9	Answer structures	108
	1.10	Sample interview questions	110

Part I

The UCAT

Overview of the UCAT

The UCAT, which stands for the **University Clinical Aptitude Test,** is an admissions test that is used as a selection criterion for most undergraduate medical, dental, oral health, and other clinical science courses offered in the United Kingdom and many other countries worldwide.

The UCAT is composed of **five multiple-choice tests** that, along with one minute for relaying instructions, each have a separate time limit. Here are a few brief descriptions of each sub-test, which we will explore in more detail in the following chapters:

- **Verbal Reasoning (44 questions, 21 minutes):** this section assesses your ability to evaluate and analyse a written passage. You either need to choose the best option from the alternatives, or decide if a given statement is true, false, or you can't tell.
- **Decision Making (29 questions, 31 minutes):** this section also looks at how you logically navigate and draw logical conclusions from stimulus and statistics that you are provided with. This may come in different forms – graphs, tables, text, or diagrams. For these questions, a calculator is available on the screen.
- **Quantitative Reasoning (36 questions, 24 minutes):** your capacity to apply numerical skills in a problem-solving setting is assessed here, largely through tables, graphs, and other forms of data. An on-screen calculator is also provided for this section.
- **Abstract Reasoning (55 questions, 13 minutes):** this component tests whether you can detect and apply patterns to different shapes, and also assesses your ability to solve non-verbal problems. They can come in the familiar form of 'Next in the Sequence' questions, but can also, for instance, ask you to sort a given shape into one of two sets.
- **Situational Judgement (69 questions, 26 mins):** this contains content that many students will find completely new, as this sub-test assesses your understanding of problems in a real-life setting and whether you can identify which course of action is most appropriate, or which factors are most important when making judgements, based on crucial situational information.

You will need to sit the UCAT around July–September if you are applying to university the following year (e.g. sitting the test in September 2026 at the start of Year 13 and then applying to university in 2027). This means that students in younger year levels, such as Year 11 or an equivalent, *cannot* sit the UCAT in advance and have their results apply to their university entry. You can also take the test as many times you want, but only once per year. However, it typically isn't necessary to sit the test early as a 'practice run' as it is better to focus on your A-Levels subjects and trust that you will be able to prepare for UCAT exam when the time comes.

If you have special testing requirements, such as an injury or disability preventing you from conventional test taking, you can sit an extended form of the UCAT, called the UCATSEN. Here, extra time or other accommodations can be arranged through an online 'Access Arrangements' application, with supporting documents. These should be submitted well in advance of the UCAT (typically the due dates are in early May for the exam in July). When you register for the UCAT, you must book your test after you get officially approved. Your UCAT mark is based around how many questions you got correct (no marks are deducted for incorrect answers), then the marks for each of the five sections are scaled, and when these are added together, they form your overall score.

The scaled mark for each of the first four sections ranges from 300 to 900, giving an overall score range from 1200 to 3600. The questions in Decision Making are worth 2 marks (i.e. 1 mark if your response is partially correct, and 2 marks if it's completely correct), while the questions for the rest of the sub-tests are work 1 mark each. For the final section, the Situational Judgement Test, full marks are given if you choose the *most* correct option and partial marks are given to an answer close to it. Rather than a score from 300 to 900, your Situational Judgement Test mark ranges from Band 1 to Band 4, where Band 1 is the highest level (which demonstrates an understanding and degree of judgement similar to the panel of experts who've written the question) and Band 4 is the lowest level (which demonstrates a degree of judgement that's vastly different).

Section 1

Section 1 – Verbal Reasoning

1.1 Introduction

The first section of the UCAT is Verbal Reasoning. As with all sections of the UCAT, this begins with one minute to read the instructions before candidates receive **21 minutes** of test-taking time. Described as an assessment of a candidate's ability to **critically evaluate information presented in a written form,** this section tests logical reasoning and problem solving. This section also assesses your ability to carefully read and consider information presented in passages, being left to determine **whether specific conclusions can be drawn from the information presented.** Furthermore, it is important to note that you are **not** expected to use prior knowledge to answer questions. The point of this sub-test is to assess your ability to understand and synthesise complex information presented in a short time period. This differs from the more traditional method used by schools and universities to assess academic merit, which generally involves content being delivered over a long period of time with the expectation that you memorise and understand it.

In order to understand how to approach the Verbal Reasoning section, it is important to grasp *why* these skills are assessed in the UCAT. One of the key aspects of being a doctor is to **process complex information** and **communicate this in a clear and simple manner to patients.** This involves interpreting findings from published materials and applying this to clinical scenarios with patients. In relation to this matter, the skill of **drawing logical conclusions** and being able to **critique the validity of findings** is hugely important. As we will elaborate on further in the core skills section of the guide, this set of skills is linked to your ability to think critically and reason logically, and thus all the questions explicitly target this.

The Verbal Reasoning section of the UCAT contains **11 passages of text** that are each around **300 words long.** Each passage has four associated questions, meaning the section has a total of **44 questions.** Given the relatively short period of time allocated for this section, it can be considered one of the more time-pressured sections of the UCAT, so practising *all* the skills involved is essential. There are two distinct types of questions that come up in the Verbal Reasoning section, and it is important to be aware of both types and have strategies to tackle each.

The first question type is colloquially known as *'True-False-Can't-Tell.'* As you might expect, this question type asks candidates to carefully read a passage and decide if a statement provided follows logically, with the options being *True, False,* and *Can't Tell.* This is often the question type that students prefer, as it is usually easier to solve these through pattern-recognition and other shortcuts, which will be elaborated on later. The second question type can prove more difficult, as it has more of a focus on **inference.** For these types, you are asked to carefully read a passage and draw conclusions from the information when presented with a question or incomplete statement. You can choose from four text response options, and you will need to pick the *best* or *most suitable* answer.

1.2 Core skills

1.2.1 Critical thinking

Critical thinking is a term thrown around a lot these days, but what exactly does it mean and how does it relate to the UCAT? Traditionally, critical thinking is defined as the process of **actively and skilfully evaluating information to reach an answer or conclusion, informed by reflective scepticism and utilising discipline.** I really do think discipline is the key word here. When reading a passage, our default setting is to draw conclusions and judge the content of the passage based on feelings and experience, tainted by bias. In daily life, there isn't necessarily a problem with this, but for the purposes of the UCAT, second-guessing your gut feeling, identifying and removing personal bias, and carefully analysing what is actually there in the passage, are all extremely important.

Thinking about this from a medical perspective, one can see why the UCAT places such an emphasis on this skill. Introducing personal bias into clinical situations can lead to the endangering of patient's lives. What separates Medicine from other health fields is that everything we do is based on sound evidence. Experiments are carefully thought out and results are published in peer-reviewed journals where other clinicians and scientists can critique aspects of the experiment. Thus, it is the responsibility of doctors is to carefully analyse evidence and make decisions in the best interests of their patients that are based on this evidence.

Of course, no one expects you to have mastered this higher-order skill by the time you are taking the UCAT. There's absolutely no need to stress over channelling your inner Socrates! The most anyone expects of you is that you start **thinking about and applying some of these principles.** The questions in the Verbal Reasoning section of the UCAT are generally considered very difficult, and with the added time pressure, it is virtually impossible to give every single question the time it requires to be answered with sound logic.

1.2.2 Logical reasoning

While critical thinking deals with establishing a thought process that removes personal bias and focuses on evidence, logical reasoning relates to your ability to carefully think through a statement in order to reach another piece of information. When discussing logical reasoning, the initial and final pieces of information are often called the **premise** and **conclusion** respectively. The process of reaching the conclusion from the premise is referred to as the **inference.**

1.2.3 Deductive reasoning

One form of logical reasoning known as **deductive reasoning** involves **linking premises with conclusions** by applying general rules until only the conclusion remains. In deductive reasoning, a chain of inference is divided into small steps so we can be sure that, if the premise is true, then the conclusion is true. This type of reasoning is commonly associated with mathematical and philosophical logic. A simple example of an argument using deductive logic is detailed as follows:

All people are mortal.
Socrates is a person.
Therefore, Socrates is a mortal.

As you can see, the first premise states that all objects in the category 'people' are assigned the attribute 'mortal.' Since the second premise classifies 'Socrates' as falling within the category of 'people,' we can therefore conclude that Socrates must be mortal as he inherits his classification as a member of the category 'people.' Deductive reasoning may seem basic and self-evident, but it is an important tool to use when tackling the Verbal Reasoning section of the UCAT. Always remember that the steps of your logic must be small and carefully thought out so as to follow the rules of deductive reasoning, as this will maximise your chances of selecting the correct answer and being able to rule out incorrect answers.

1.2.4 Inductive reasoning

Inductive reasoning contrasts with deductive reasoning as it involves multiple premises that are found to be true *most* of the time and so are combined to obtain a specific conclusion. Whilst the conclusion of a deductive argument is a *certainty*, the conclusion of an inductive argument may only be *probable*, given the evidence provided. An example of an inductive argument is provided below:

All cats you have observed purr.
Therefore, every cat must purr.

The conclusion that 'every cat must purr' is not defined as valid or invalid, as would be the case with deductive reasoning, but rather strong or weak, which describes how probable the conclusion is.

1.2.5 Abductive reasoning

Abductive reasoning can be considered a form of inductive reasoning, as it involves the use of multiple premises to obtain a conclusion; however, it employs explanations to describe *how* the premises are linked to the conclusion, and is thus often required in questions asking you to find the 'best explanation' for something. In modern medical practice, the process of abductive reasoning is essentially producing a model that explains the sum total of a data set better than any other model, allowing us to conclude that the model is probably correct. As you can imagine, this process is used by doctors and scientists on a daily basis, and is preferred to inductive reasoning, as being confined only to statistical reasoning does not allow us to reach the best or most logical conclusion in every case. This relates to a concept that is a key focus of the Verbal Reasoning section of the UCAT:

Correlation does not equal causation!

Correlation is defined as a measure that indicates the extent to which one object is associated with another, while **causation** describes how an act or agent can produce an effect in another object. While the definitions appear to be distinctive, the UCAT will try and trick you into mixing up the two, so it is very important to carefully read the information given and never extrapolate a cause and effect relationship. A common example of how data can be misinterpreted is detailed as follows:

Ice cream sales increase during summer.
Incidences of sunburn also increase in summer.
Therefore an increase in ice cream sales causes sunburn.

Obviously the conclusion that "an increase in ice cream sales causes sunburn" is incorrect, however exclusively looking at the data would suggest this. One clear issue with this inference is that it completely ignores the fact that both ice cream sales and incidences of sunburn increase during summer. In this case, summer is referred to as a **confounding variable** as it is not accounted for and can suggest correlation when in fact there is no logical explanation for such findings.

1.2.6 Reading proficiency and speed reading

Reading and evaluating a wide range of written information is a very important skill for medical students and healthcare practitioners. As medical information is becoming more accessible, there is a greater need to distinguish trustworthy sources and spot unsound inferences. Developing the critical thinking and logical reasoning skills we have already detailed will equip you with the toolkit necessary to digest and scrutinise many forms of information, however becoming proficient in reading is equally as vital. While the skill of reading may not appear to be as important as these higher order skills, technical mastery can prove essential for UCAT success.

One strategy that will significantly help you in the Verbal Reasoning section is learning to **speed read.** While this skill remains somewhat controversial in the scientific world, there is no doubt that increasing your reading speed is beneficial for the purposes of the UCAT. As we have mentioned, the Verbal Reasoning section involves serious time pressure, and giving yourself more time to think through each section can allow you to maximise your marks. There are three types of reading you should understand before delving into this topic.

1. The first type is probably what you are using now to read these words, and is known as **mental reading.** Mental readers generally read at about 250 words per minute and use **subvocalization,** which involves sounding each word out inside your head. The issue with subvocalization is that it limits your reading speed to how fast you can talk, as you need to say every word inside your head in order to understand it.
2. The next method is **auditory reading,** where you hear words read out as you read them. This is a faster process and auditory readers can read at approximately 450 words per minute.
3. Finally, there is **visual reading,** where you understand the meaning of a word without sounding or hearing it. This is the fastest process and allows you to reach reading speeds of 700 words per minute; however, it can be a difficult skill to cultivate.

Studies have shown that completely eliminating subvocalization is not possible, however there are many strategies available to **minimise subvocalization** and become more of a visual reader. Reading is not about the words themselves, but about extracting ideas, and many words such as 'a' and 'an' only have a grammatical purpose and therefore can be left out without compromising understanding of the passage.

Meta guiding is the most common strategy to increase reading speed by minimising subvocalization. This involves the visual guiding of the eye by using a finger or pointer to force the eye to move faster along the length of a passage of text.

Skimming is also another technique employed by speed readers, and involves searching through sentences for key words and concepts, and especially looking through the beginning and end of a passage where the author may explain their ideas. However, this method is *not* ideal for the purposes of the UCAT, as it may lead to assumptions being made regarding the content of the passage, which is exactly what you *don't* want to do in Section 1! The meta guiding strategy is a much more suitable tool for getting through the passages, as it does not fundamentally change your method of reading, and should be able to give you a boost to your reading speed without requiring extreme dedication.

Of course, you should absolutely practise reading using meta guiding in the lead up to the UCAT if you plan on using the strategy to ensure no comprehension is lost, as at the end of the day, **comprehension is more important than speed.** If you don't plan on using the strategy, that is okay as well. For some people, their time may be better spent preparing in other ways, and increasing your reading speed is not the only way to succeed in the Verbal Reasoning section of the UCAT.

Even if you don't plan on increasing your reading speed, making a habit of reading non-fiction passages in the lead up to the UCAT is highly beneficial. Try picking up a newspaper or reading a science article each day. This will get you used to reading long passages with sometimes abstract ideas, which will make up the questions in the UCAT Verbal Reasoning section. When you are doing this, try to make a dot point summary of the passage from memory and see how strong your understanding, comprehension, and retention of the text is. Practising this skill over a period of time will greatly improve your efficiency and accuracy when you are sitting the test.

With regards to reading, attention to detail is a key to solving many questions and can be an often overlooked aspect. For instance, if the passage says "cats are sometimes cute", and then the questions asks if "cats are always cute," then you know that it's not technically correct. Subtle changes in the wording of questions can provide very useful clues, sometimes allowing you to quickly choose the correct answer or discard an incorrect answer without having to ponder the content of the passage. The questions will always be based on what is explicitly mentioned in the passage, so as have previously said you should not apply any of your own knowledge or assumptions to answering Verbal Reasoning questions.

1.3 General advice for Section 1

1.3.1 How to prepare

The first thing to do when you are starting to prepare for the Verbal Reasoning section of the UCAT is to work out a general strategy. There are many ways to approach this section and we will outline several methods designed to maximise your marks, but ultimately your approach should come down to personal choice. Try to first practise a few questions and think about which strategies would suit your style of working through the Verbal Reasoning section. Once you find an effective strategy, stick with it! There is no point in wasting your time playing around with multiple strategies only to end up mastering none of them. Keep using your strategy while practising questions until it becomes second nature. Your dedication will be rewarded as this gives you the best possible chance of attaining a high score in the Verbal Reasoning section.

The next thing you should do is to continue practising questions, but now under **timed conditions.** One of the biggest challenges of this section is the time pressure, so once you have committed to an approach, there is no point in continuing to do untimed questions. You should aim to replicate the conditions of the exam by giving yourself **21 minutes** to do **44 questions.**

A common mistake people make when preparing for the UCAT is to spend more time doing practice questions than *marking* them, when in fact you should be doing the opposite. Practice questions are only useful if you can learn from your experience, so you should thoroughly mark your answers and carefully look through detailed solutions in order to fully understand how to complete the question correctly. This extends not only to questions you got wrong, but questions you got right as well, as you may have used an incorrect method, or simply guessed. The solutions may also explain something about the question or solution you aren't yet aware of. If you do this method correctly, it will greatly improve your critical thinking and reasoning skills as you will begin to understand the inner workings of questions in the Verbal Reasoning section, allowing you to see patterns in how they are structured. This can open up opportunities to answer the questions much quicker, especially for the easier and more formulaic questions.

1.3.2 Tips for staying on time

In the Verbal Reasoning section of the UCAT, you are given approximately 30 seconds to complete each of the 44 questions, making it very important to stay on time. In the following few paragraphs, we will outline some strategies for minimising time wastage through having a robust process for answering each question and knowing how to deal with difficult questions.

For the Verbal Reasoning section, it is very important to **read the questions carefully before reading the passage.** It may seem intuitive to read the passage first as it comes before the actual set of four associated questions, however if you read the passage afterwards, it speeds up the process as you can skim through looking for key words and ideas relating to the questions and ignore material that is irrelevant. Reading the passage first is also problematic as you won't know what to look for so you may not be able to recall a specific section of the passage when you reach the questions.

The UCAT likes to throw long and dense Verbal Reasoning passages at you. Often these can be slightly ambiguous and it will be tempting to hesitate and overthink the questions. The key here is to **completely avoid overthinking anything!** Verbal Reasoning questions require clear and simple logical reasoning, so getting into a convoluted chain of thought will not only confuse you, but waste precious time. The questions themselves often aren't too difficult – it's just that you can be thrown off by irrelevant complexities of the passage.

When you read the question for a second time after going through the passage, it is also a good idea to have a scan through the possible answers. This is where attention to detail with regards to reading can come into play. As mentioned in the section on reading proficiency, if you notice a subtle flaw in an answer, you can discard that answer and focus on the remaining ones. It is important to be ruthless in doing this, as crossing off even one answer increases your chances of getting the question right by a substantial amount, and allows you to not have to consider that option if you need to revisit the question later, thus saving you time. On the flip side, if you see an answer that is clearly correct, just select it and move on. Looking at the other answers will be a waste of time and may plant doubts in your mind that further slow you down.

If you have narrowed it down to two options, make a quick decision. It's tempting to spend a lengthy amount of time weighing up both options, but in the end it's a 50-50 chance, so the best thing you can do in this situation is to pick one and move on. Spending more time agonising over the decision will probably not make you any more likely to choose the correct answer and you will be missing out on potentially easy marks further along in the section.

The UCAT is bound to throw some difficult questions at you, not only to challenge your reasoning abilities, but also to slow you down and see how well you cope with being thrown a curveball. When you come across a **difficult Verbal Reasoning question,** it may seem impossible to crack open at first; however, if you want to have any chance of solving it, you must avoid getting flustered and accept that it may take a bit longer. We know it's difficult to put your mind at ease when time is ticking away and you aren't making any progress, but developing a positive mindset in these scenarios is essential! With that being said, you obviously don't want to waste too much time on the difficult questions, and if you feel like you're not getting anywhere, make an educated guess and keep moving forward.

1.3.3 Running out of time

Even if you apply every strategy for staying on time, there is still a very real possibility you will be left with too many questions and not enough time. It can be daunting being left with five minutes to complete as many as 20 questions, but it is important to know you can still finish the section and do well if you change up your strategy. When you reach this stage, there's no time for perfectionism. Everything is about **maximising your chances of picking the right answer** in as little time as possible, so be ruthless and don't waste time checking your answers.

The key to all this is making **educated guesses.** These are never ideal, but they are significantly better than random guesses when done right.

- The first thing you should do is **read the question** and then skim through the passage looking for **useful key words.** Your understanding probably won't be great, but it might be enough to use common sense and your gut feeling to find an answer you feel is right.
- You should also **analyse the language used in the answers.** If you find **superlative language** (i.e. extreme words) such as 'biggest,' 'always,' and 'definitely,' the answer is more likely to be incorrect as the examiners like to trip people up by extending statements from the passage too far.
- On the other hand, **low modal language** (i.e. mild words) such as 'should,' 'sometimes,' and 'might' generally indicate the answer is correct as they are more inclusive and thus more likely to match the information stated in the passage.

1.4 Strategy for *True-False-Can't-Tell* questions

As you may recall, the first question type that appears in the UCAT Verbal Reasoning section gives you the options *True, False,* and *Can't Tell.* While this question type is thought to be less favoured by exam-sitters, it still has an important part to play, and you should exploit these questions to gain more time to tackle the more difficult type of question (i.e. the free text questions that we'll talk about next). In the following section, we will go into more depth about how to approach *True-False-Can't-Tell* Questions and provide examples on how to successfully work through them.

1.4.1 Defining *True*, *False* and *Can't Tell*

Before you begin to practise questions and apply the skills you have learned, it is important to understand what the three possible answers really mean, allowing you to differentiate between them. The options *True*, *False* and *Can't Tell* have certain connotations and as soon as you know what these are, you can more easily distinguish between them when looking at a passage, thus greatly improving your accuracy and efficiency.

- A statement is ***True*** if the same information in the statement is found **explicitly stated in the passage.** Typically the information is directly stated somewhere, albeit usually in a **rephrased form** using synonyms. Sometimes the information may not be directly stated in the passage, however you can **validate that it is correct** by bringing together various pieces found in different places in the passage. A statement can also be *True* if there is enough content within the passage to **make an inference.** This can be a grey area as using inferences does bring in the possibility that *Can't Tell* is the correct option; however, if it seems like you have followed a rigorous and logical train of thought to validate the statement, then *True* is the best response. You must also be careful not to bring in any external information though, as if you bring in your own general knowledge, it can compromise your thought process. Always assume that **only the passage can supply facts and information that influence your decisions.**

- A statement is ***False*** if the information in the statement is **directly contradicted** by what is stated in the passage. If you find any piece of information within the passage that contradicts the statement, you can safely select *False* as your answer. It is important to look for **subtle changes in wording,** as a sneaky negative may trip you up. Much like with the *True* category, you can infer that the statement is *False*, however again it can be a grey area. You should also keep in mind that just because the passage says something different to the passage, it does not necessarily make it *False*. As long as the passage is not directly contradicted, *Can't Tell* remains an option, as the varying information may not be conflicting. Another common reason for statement to be *False*, is for it to take something in the passage and extend it too far. For example, the passage may state, "The company Kookaburra is one of the few Australian cricket bat manufacturers", while the statement may say, "Kookaburra is the only Australian cricket bat manufacturer". In this case the statement is *False* as while it follows the logic of the passage but takes it too far and is **factually incorrect according to what is stated in the passage.**

- In any case where *True* and *False* do not seem to be valid options, ***Can't Tell*** is likely the right answer. If you select this option it means the information in the statement **doesn't appear in the text** or you are **unable to infer** whether the statement is *True* or *False*. This can often be one of the most difficult answers to correctly as you will not be able to find anything explicitly stated in the passage. In many cases, the information goes beyond what is stated in the passage. For example, the passage may say "Scotland has <u>one of the best</u> medical schools in the UK," while the statement may say "Scotland has <u>the best</u> medical school in the UK." For all we know, the statement could very well be correct, however **the passage does not give us enough information,** so *Can't Tell* is the answer. Much like the other options, something you need to watch out for is that you don't bring any personal knowledge to the question – the information in the passage is all you need!

Now that you have covered the basics of this question type, it is time to go through an example. Factual passages like the one that follows are quite common in the Verbal Reasoning section of the UCAT, so you should get used to reading and evaluating scientific articles. If you are interested in practising analysis of pieces like this, you should consider finding reputable websites which publish regular summaries of advances in science and technology.

1.4 Strategy for True-False-Can't-Tell questions

SAMPLE:

Cancer is an illness that remains a challenge to many scientists and medical practitioners. Finding new and effective treatments that destroy cancer cells without affecting the rest of the body has been a struggle, however this may soon be changing. Human trials are scheduled to begin for a new cancer treatment that employs the body's own immune system to attack cancer cells. The research institute that devised the trial plans on implanting edited immune system cells from strangers to fight tumours rather than more traditional cancer treatments such as chemotherapy. In interviews, the scientists behind the project explained it as a DIY approach to cancer therapy. Instead of relying on chemicals or radiation to fight tumours, the transplants aim to equip the bodies of cancer patients with the tools to fight tumours on their own. It is believed these trials could lead to a whole new approach doctors could use to fight cancer. These new developments in reprogramming the immune system have caused experts to speculate that 20 years from now, the vast majority of cancers will either be rapidly treated diseases or long-term chronic issues that can be managed by a doctor. While this seems distant, the therapy has already offered hope to many current sufferers of cancer and survivors who fear a second cancer.

- **Statement 1:** "The DIY approach to cancer therapy reprograms cells of the patient's immune system to fight tumours."
  This statement is a test of your reading and comprehension skills. While the first sentence states that the cancer treatment "employs the body's own immune system to attack cancer cells," you have to be careful as later in the paragraph it states that "immune system cells from strangers" are implanted, so you can infer that that these cells from other people are the ones being reprogrammed. Thus the answer is *False*.

- **Statement 2:** "Experts believe this new approach to cancer therapy will mean that all cancers will be able to be rapidly treated or managed as a long-term condition within the next 20 years."
  If you rush and don't carefully reread the relevant section of the passage, this statement could trip you up. If you look again, you will see the passage states that some have speculated that "20 years from now, the vast majority of cancers will either be rapidly treated diseases or long-term chronic issues that can be managed by a doctor." Thus, *False* is the correct answer.
  It is frustrating to get these basic questions wrong, so you have to stay on the ball and look out for subtle changes in wording. Even if you were in a rush, you should also be able to pick up the extreme wording in the statement. Saying something about all cancers" is a sweeping generalisation regardless of the content of the passage, so you would be more likely to get the question correct by selecting *False* as the answer.

- **Statement 3:** "The DIY approach to cancer therapy is more effective than chemotherapy."
  You may infer that given the "vast majority of cancers will either be rapidly treated diseases or long-term chronic issues," the new cancer therapy can be considered more effective than chemotherapy. This, however, is an incorrect assumption. Within the Verbal Reasoning section, you are allowed to assume anything stated in the passage by the author is a fact, but in this case, the evidence in the passage is speculation from experts in the field, and is considered an opinion. Thus there are no grounds to infer that the statement is *True*. This does not necessarily mean that the statement is *False* either, particularly since there are no explicit contradictions. Nothing in the passage directly compares chemotherapy and the new cancer therapy, and thus the correct answer is *Can't Tell*, as the information in the statement goes beyond the text.

- **Statement 4:** "Doctors do not currently use this approach for treating cancer."
  This statement is a fair bit simpler than the preceding three. It requires the basic inference that if "these trials could lead to a whole new approach doctors could use to fight cancer," then doctors are not currently using this approach for treating cancer. Thus the correct answer is *True*. It is not uncommon for easy marks to be hidden at the end of question sets. This is why you shouldn't be too concerned about spending more time working through the first question in a set, as any additional understanding you get about the passage will help you answer the other questions from the set quicker.

1.4 Strategy for True-False-Can't-Tell questions

The next passage is more challenging as it is quite wordy and lengthy. With these kinds of texts, reading the questions first is essential so you can select a key word and search for it in the passage to quickly find the answer. If you feel you have difficulty with passages like this, you can practise quickly scanning through long passages by reading newspaper articles and testing your comprehension afterwards.

> **SAMPLE:**
>
> *Video gaming is currently a highly popular form of entertainment, with gamers around the world collectively spending around 4 billion hours per week in front of their screens. When considering this enormous number, it comes as no surprise that there is an increasing amount of research being undertaken to examine the impact of video gaming on brain. At a glance, more than 60% of UK people aged 16+ play video games for at least 2 hours per week. The average age of video gamers is 28. With regards to children playing video games, 67% of parents indicate that video games have had a positive influence on their child's life.*
>
> *Video game sales have continued to increase every year. In 2023, the industry sales exceeded US$184 billion. The top three best-selling video games of the year were The Legend of Zelda, Baldur's Gate 3, and Super Mario Bros Wonder. One of the most popular gaming genres is the First Person Shooter or Action-Adventure games, which have often been accused of promoting aggressive and violent behaviour along with causing video game addiction. Scientists have spent countless years researching the link between video gaming and violence, failing to reach a consensus. While there have been heated debates about this topic with passionate activists on both sides, the only thing to be said at this stage is that there is no causal link between playing video games and committing acts of violence in the real world.*
>
> *Yet this is not the only effect of video games that scientists have spent time extensively studying. There is evidence to suggest that video gaming affects the brain in a variety of ways and can even cause changes in certain regions of the brain. Scientists have recently collected and summarised results from 116 scientific studies to determine how video games influence our brains and behaviours. The studies included in the review show that gamers display improvements in several types of attention, including sustained attention and selective attention. Furthermore, the regions of the brain that play a role in attention are more efficient in gamers compared with non-gamers, and they requires less activation to stay focused on demanding tasks. Evidence also demonstrates that playing video games in the long-term increases the size and competence of parts of the brain responsible for visuospatial skills, which allow us to mentally manipulate and analyse objects in three dimensions. Stimulation of these areas have shown promise in providing protection against dementia and Alzheimer's disease.*
>
> *The effect of video games on the brain is a new area of research that will continue to be explored. We may just be scraping the surface of the potential that video games could present in enhancing cognitive ability.*
>
> - **Statement 1:** "The public are spending around 4 billion hours consuming on-screen media."
>   You should find the key word "4 billion" with relative ease by skimming through the first paragraph. If you read the sentence carefully, you will realise that video gamers, not the general public, are spending this amount of time in front of their screens. It is clear from this statistic that the amount of hours the public spend consuming all on-screen media, notably including television and movies, must exceed 4 billion, and thus the correct answer is *False*.
> - **Statement 2:** "First Person Shooter and Action-Adventure games do not promote acts of violence." The initial piece of information we receive about statement within the passage is that these genres are often "accused of promoting aggressive and violent behaviour." Obviously, this doesn't give us any ability to say with confidence whether the statement is *True* or *False*, however it suggests a correlation. In the proceeding sentences, you may infer the lack of causal link between video games and aggression as evidence that these games do not promote acts of violence, however scientists have not reached a consensus, and thus the answer is *Can't Tell*.

- **Statement 3:** "Individuals who regularly play video games find it easier to remain on task compared to non-gamers."

  This statement tests your ability to synthesise information and assess the validity of a conclusion. The conclusion drawn by the statement may seem like a bit of a reach, however there is plenty of evidence for it in the passage. According to the text, gamers show improved "sustained attention and selective attention," along with more efficiency in certain areas of the brain, requiring "less activation to stay focused on demanding tasks." Remember, you can't bring any external knowledge into your reasoning process and you must think critically to ensure you are not being biased. Given the evidence, the statement is *True*, as increased ability to remain on task is definitely comparable to the information given in the passage relating to improved attention and focus.

- **Statement 4:** "Symptoms of dementia and Alzheimer's disease may include signs of reduced visuospatial skills."

  This is a tougher statement that needs to be analysed through reversing some of the logic presented in the passage. We know that the areas of the brain responsible for visuospatial skills can be stimulated to protect against dementia and Alzheimer's disease, which would imply that these conditions affect the visuospatial regions of the brain and thus should impair the associated skills. While this inference is substantiated by the evidence, it is a large logical leap and favours the answer *Can't Tell*, however the statement is fairly mild, including the key word "may," which means that the answer is *True*. In general, if you see a statement with mild language, there is leeway to be a bit more liberal with your inferences to truth, whereas extreme language places very harsh restrictions on the information that must be seen in the passage to prove truth.

1.5 Strategy for Free Text questions

The second type of question found in the Verbal Reasoning section of the UCAT is called Free Text, as the answer options are not limited to *True*, *False*, and *Can't Tell*. As there are more answer possibilities, this question type is generally considered more difficult and time-consuming, and also forms the majority of Verbal Reasoning questions. Within this question category, there is another subdivision – some questions have a specific question within the stem, providing four similar statements which you have to choose from, while other questions have a generic statement within the stem, and you have choose between four unrelated statements. In the next few pages of the guide, we will go into detail about what you can expect with Free Text questions before providing some examples to demonstrate various strategies.

1.5.1 How to approach questions with a specific stem

In general, Free Text questions are more challenging than *True-False-Can't Tell* questions as there are four unfamiliar statements to read through compared to the three familiar options. This adds another level of complexity and time pressure as there are more ways to trip up and more options you have to eliminate before reaching the answer. The good thing about questions with a specific stem is that **all statements will share a theme,** as they are all trying to convince you that they are the correct answer to the specific question. This means that it in most cases it should be easy to pick a key word or idea from the question stem as it will be common to all the options. Searching for the relevant statements in the passage and finding information to eliminate options you think are incorrect can really be the key here. Unlike *True-False-Can't-Tell* questions, where you really have to find the evidence to select the correct answer, for Free Text questions, it can be quicker to find the evidence to eliminate all incorrect statements until you are left with the correct answer.

The following passage is an example of a text centred around a writer's comment or opinion on a topic. One of the key things to remember for these kinds of texts is that you have to focus on the author's opinion, rather than exclusively on statistics or facts. In order to save time, it is best to have a **glance at the conclusion of the text before you begin,** as it will often have the key information summarised by the writer. If you are looking for material to practise with, most newspapers should have opinion or comment sections which you can use to test your skills in analysing a piece and extracting the author's key points and opinions.

1.5 Strategy for Free Text questions

SAMPLE:

It's taken a while, but the hype around continually upgrading smartphones is finally dying, as Apple revealed sobering data from their latest quarterly report. The truth behind Apple's alarming news of weak iPhone sales is that the tech industry has hit Peak Smartphone, a tipping point when everyone who can afford one already owns one and no breakthroughs in technology are compelling them to upgrade as frequently as in previous years. Some manufacturers have boosted prices to keep up profit, but Apple's shortfall demonstrates the limits of employing this strategy. Most major smartphone companies have been rightly criticised for their lack of creative innovations, and many consumers are happy to see them suffering from this, hoping it will spur on progress.

The company said demand for iPhones is waning, and revenue for the last quarter of 2018 falls well below projections, a decrease that has been traced to China. Apple's shares dropped 10 per cent following the news, which is its worst loss since 2013. This news has been seen as a wakeup call for the industry, however it's not just Apple that has been suffering losses. Demand has been lacklustre across the board, and Samsung, the leading seller of smartphones, have been hit even harder with an 8 per cent drop in phone shipments across the last 12 months.

Smartphone makers used to be like teenagers, and the industry was on fire. Now it feels like they're more like senior citizens in terms of maturity. Apple's iPhone is its most expensive yet, but it's not making up for the drop in sales. Innovations in smartphone technology grew in leaps and bounds in the early 2010s, but now it has slowed down, and consumers are less inclined to make the upgrade each year. Maybe it's time for new company with bright ideas to steal the spotlight.

Question: The author suggests that which of the following has been the cause for the recent drop in iPhone sales?

- **Option 1:** The new iPhone is too expensive for many consumers.
  While the passage does mention that "Apple's iPhone is its most expensive yet," there is no information to infer that this is the cause for the recent drop in iPhone sales, as it appears in the passage to be more of a compensatory measure due to the decrease in sales.
- **Option 2:** The Chinese market has lost interest in smartphones.
  It is certainly evident from the passage that the drop in iPhone demand has been "traced back to China," so it is a fair assumption that the Chinese market has been the cause for the drop in iPhone sales. The issue with this option is that there is no mention within the passage of anyone, let alone Chinese consumers, losing interest in iPhones. There could be a number of factors influencing this market, so based on the information within the text, it is too much of a reach to infer that this option is correct.
- **Option 3:** Innovations in smartphone technology have slowed down.
  In the first paragraph, the author says that we have reached "Peak Smartphone" due in part to the lack of technological breakthroughs in the sector. This opinion is reinforced later in the passage when the writer states that innovations have slowed down since the 2010s, and this means that consumers are less inclined to upgrade their phone. Evidently, this provides strong evidence for the author believing this to be the reason for the drop in iPhone sales. It is particularly important to note that this information is featured in the conclusion, which is often when author's put forth their strongest opinions. Thus, this is the correct option.
- **Option 4:** iPhone owners who have been loyal to Apple are now deciding to make the switch to other companies such as Samsung.
  This option is very easy to rule out if you have read the passage. The text mentions that "demand has been lacklustre across the board", and that Samsung has been "hit even harder" than Apple, so clearly this is incorrect. Often it can be useful to have a general sense of the passage through skim reading, as being able to quickly rule out obviously false answers greatly increases your chance of getting the question right within the time constraints.

1.5.2 How to approach questions with a generic stem

Questions with a generic stem are the most difficult kind of question you will find in the Verbal Reasoning section of the UCAT. Questions with a specific stem can often be answered by examining a small piece of information within the passage and using it to rule out enough options to select the correct answer. Unfortunately, this is not the case for questions with a generic stem, as the statements to pick from can be unrelated, making the question more confusing. To top it off, the information to infer whether each statement is correct or incorrect can be found in **different areas of the passage,** and may require **several different key words or ideas** to quickly locate.

Occasionally, two statements may be related, so it will be possible to use the same key word to identify information in the passage relating to the statements. As you want to find the correct answer as quickly as possible, and preferably without searching through all the options, **start with the option you feel has the best chance of being correct.** This may not always be reliable, but at the very least it will be more efficient than always starting with the first option.

When facing the Verbal Reasoning section, it is very important to have a **flexible mindset!** The following passage presents a different kind of text to show that the UCAT can always have some surprises in store. It also has plenty of juicy key words you can use to skim for when trying to analyse each answer, which is an imperative skill to have for questions with a generic stem. Don't be too concerned about practising analysis of this particular style of writing, as most passages in Verbal Reasoning will fall into the more conventional major categories – you just want to be aware that the UCAT can throw you curve-balls like this and that there will be at least one or two unique kinds of passages.

1.5 Strategy for Free Text questions

SAMPLE :
Our glamorous journey begins as your flight arrives at Reykjavik airport and you are transferred to your accommodation for a brief one-night stay. Our search for the Northern Lights begins the next morning and we head out into the gorgeous countryside for our expedition, leaving the city lights behind us for the best chance at witnessing this spectacular natural phenomenon. We make a stop at Eldhestar horse park for dinner and there is an optional upgrade to view a native Icelandic horse show, before settling down for a cosy night in the town of Hella.

Now it is the second day, we travel through the farmlands and mountains of southern Iceland, a region well-known due to its description in a famous 13th century heroic Saga, which imbues it with a sense of historical significance. We pass the stunning snow-capped volcanoes of Hekla and Eyjafjallajökull on our way. We also stop at the quaint village of Skógar to visit the Folk Museum, with its collection of restored turf-roofed houses, and pass the Sólheimajökull glacier before returning to Hella.

On the third and final day, we enjoy a tour of Iceland's Golden Circle, relishing some of the country's most incredible natural wonders, including the magnificent two-tiered Golden Falls at Gullfoss. We also visit Þingvellir National Park, a UNESCO World Heritage Site, home to a dramatic canyon running through the park which is the dividing fault line between two of Earth's tectonic plates. Later, we return to Reykjavik to conclude our journey.

Question: Which of the following would the author most likely agree with?

- **Option 1:** It is easy to view the Northern Lights from the city."
  The author mentions that the tour leaves the city for the "best chance" at witnessing the Northern Lights. This implies that it is still possible to see them from the city, however it will be difficult due to light pollution, thus making this an incorrect option.
- **Option 2:** It is worth upgrading the tour to see the Icelandic horse show at Eldhestar.
  Thus, writer briefly discusses the optional upgrade to view an Icelandic horse show at Eldhestar, but does not make any comment about the quality of the show or whether it was worth it. Thus, this too is an incorrect option.
- **Option 3:** The Sólheimajökull glacier is the most superb part of the journey.
  Immediately this option should seem suspicious. Language such as "most superb" is quite extreme, particularly since the author uses excessively positive language to describe most of the trip. If you do look at the relevant section of the passage, you will find that the writer does no use any adjective to describe this site, so clearly there are no grounds to infer that this option is correct.
- **Option 4:** The farmlands and mountains of southern Iceland provide a backdrop for reflection on the impact of the scenery on the native inhabitants.
  If you come to the last option and have completely ruled out all the other options, you should probably select it and move on, however it is always good to be thorough, and sometimes a quick check can save you some marks. In this case, it may be a bit confusing, as this option is rather ambiguous. The section of the passage that mentions "the farmlands and mountains of southern Iceland" comments on how it was described in a "13th century heroic saga" and gives the location "historical significance." While it may seem like a stretch to equate this with providing a "backdrop for reflection on the impact of the scenery on the native inhabitants", you have to remember that Verbal Reasoning questions are all about selecting the best answer, and sometimes that means the selecting the answer that *isn't incorrect*.

Well that's it for the first section of the UCAT! Verbal Reasoning is tough, but we hope the skills and strategies we have outlined, along with the examples of how to use them, have helped you gain insight into how to succeed in this section. We have provided two sample passages and question sets following this so you can develop an even greater understanding of how Verbal Reasoning questions are designed to test you.

1.6 Sample questions

SAMPLE:
The Great Barrier Reef is on the verge of being wiped out, and there is very little hope of its massive dead zones ever springing back to life, scientists have warned. The natural wonder has been hit by a series of mass bleaching incidents which have tragically turned the reefs into barren underwater wastelands. An aerial survey of the entire 2,300 km-long reef, which once was one of the most biodiverse places in the world, confirmed fears that continued mass bleaching events on a yearly basis will offer zero prospect of recovery from the high levels of coral loss.

Bleaching occurs when corals are put under stress by warming sea water or some other threat, which causes them to expel the algae that live in their tissue. In this case, record-breaking temperatures driven by global warming have been responsible for the bleaching. It is particularly concerning that mass bleaching is occurring even without the assistance of El Niño, the natural climate cycle in the Pacific Ocean.

The Barrier Reef is already under pressure from farming run-off, development, and crown-of-thorns starfish, which prey on coral. Tropical storms and cyclones have also wreaked havoc. Clearly the reef is struggling due compounding effects from many sources, however the most pressing of these issues is doubtlessly global warming. Ultimately, we need to cut carbon emissions, and the window to do so is rapidly closing.

1. **Most of the biodiversity in the Great Barrier Reef has been wiped out by mass bleaching.**
   (a) True
   (b) False
   (c) Can't Tell
2. **Coral only expel the algae within their tissue due to warming of sea water.**
   (a) True
   (b) False
   (c) Can't Tell
3. **El Niño causes a cyclical rise in Australian sea water temperature.**
   (a) True
   (b) False
   (c) Can't Tell
4. **Tropical storms and cyclones have been responsible for most of the reef's destruction.**
   (a) True
   (b) False
   (c) Can't Tell

SAMPLE :

Coffee is a huge aspect of Ethiopia's history, culture, and mythology. There are a number of legends surrounding the discovery of coffee, with Yemen also having a set of myths to lay claim to the title of being the origin of coffee. In Ethiopia, this cultural significance dates back to the ninth century when coffee cultivation began. In terms of myth, an Abyssinian goat herder by the name Kaldi is said to have discovered coffee in the form of cherries. When he was herding his goats near a monastery, he noticed they were jumping around in an excited manner, and found that the source of excitement was a small shrub with bright red cherries. Overcome with curiosity, he tried the berries himself and was astounded by their energising effects.

He decided to bring the berries to the monastery to share them with the monks, believing they would enjoy these heaven-sent delights. Upon his arrival, the coffee beans were not greeted with elation, but with disdain. One of the monks called them the work of the Devil and tossed them in a fire. According to legend, the aroma of the roasted beans was enough to make the monks give the beans a second chance. They removed the coffee beans from the fire, and crushed them before placing them in hot water for preservation. All the monks in the monastery smelled the aroma of the coffee and came to try it. These monks found that the coffee's effects were beneficial in keeping them awake during their spiritual prayers and holy devotions, vowing to drink this newfound beverage each day.

The legend of Kaldi suggests that coffee was discovered as a stimulant and as a beverage on the same day. Historical evidence, however, suggests it is far more likely that the beans were chewed as a stimulant for centuries before becoming a beverage. The beans may have been ground and mixed with ghee, a form of clarified butter, to form a nutritious thick paste. This would have been rolled into small balls which could be consumed as needed on long journeys. Today, the tradition of consuming coffee ground in ghee remains in many areas of Ethiopia. Some people also add a little melted clarified butter to their brewed coffee. Gradually, coffee became known beyond Ethiopia. Around the thirteenth century, coffee spread to the Islamic world, where it was revered as a potent medicine and powerful prayer aid. It was boiled for intensity and strength much like many medicinal concoctions. You can still find traditions of boiling coffee in Ethiopia, Turkey and much of the Mediterranean.

1. **Which of the following can be inferred from the passage?**
   (a) Coffee was being cultivated in 850 AD.
   (b) Adding clarified butter to brewed coffee increases its nutritional value.
   (c) Coffee is a powerful medicinal remedy.
   (d) In the legend of Kaldi, the monks place the roasted and crushed beans in hot water because they want to taste coffee.

2. **Which of the following statements is true?**
   (a) In the legend of Kaldi, Kaldi discovers coffee through his goats.
   (b) Coffee does not originate from Ethiopia.
   (c) Boiling coffee enhances the flavour.
   (d) The Islamic world initially scorned the arrival of coffee.

3. **In the legend of Kaldi, why did Kaldi bring the cherries to the monks?**
   (a) The cherries were found near their monastery.
   (b) He knew the monks needed coffee to maintain their energy for their prayers.
   (c) He thought coffee would be an excellent medicine.
   (d) He believed the cherries were delivered to him by God.

4. **Based on historical evidence, how did coffee become a beverage?**
   (a) It was mixed with ghee to form a thick paste for consumption on long journeys.
   (b) Monks tried to preserve coffee beans in hot water.
   (c) When it spread to the Islamic world, coffee was boiled to increase its strength as a medical remedy.
   (d) In Turkey, coffee was made into a beverage as it tasted better in a liquid form.

1.7 Answers to sample questions

Question 1: C

We know the reef was once "one of the most biodiverse places in the world," however we don't know how much of that biodiversity has been wiped out by mass bleaching as the passage mostly comments on coral dying.

Question 2: B

As the passage states, coral also release their algae in response to stress from other causes.

Question 3: A

El Niño is described as a climate cycle, so it is fair to assume that it influences temperatures in the Pacific Ocean, and by extension, the Great Barrier Reef. The fact that mass bleaching has occurred without El Niño implies that El Niño functions somewhat similarly to global warming, increasing sea water temperatures.

Question 4: C

We know that the storms and cyclones have "wreaked havoc", but there is no indication that their damage is more severe than other factors such as climate change. Climate change is also described as the "most pressing", which cannot be equated with causing the most damage, ruling out *False* as an answer.

Question 5: B

It can be inferred that adding clarified butter increases nutrition as in the passage it mentions that before coffee became a beverage, it was ground up with ghee, a form of clarified butter, to form a nutritious paste.

Question 6: A

It is stated at the start of the passage that Kaldi first observes the effects of coffee through his goats.

Question 7: D

Kaldi believes the berries to be "heaven-sent," which implies he brings them to the monks as he thinks they are delivered to him by God.

Question 8: C

The only indication in the passage of how, based on historical evidence, coffee becomes a beverage is through being boiled as a medicine upon arriving in the Islamic world.

Section 2

Section 2 – Decision Making

2.1 Introduction

Decision Making is the second section of the UCAT, and begins with one minute to read the instructions before the 31 minutes of test-taking time starts. This section is described as an assessment of your ability to **apply logic to reach a decision or conclusion, evaluate arguments, and analyse statistical information.** The actual core skills required for this section resemble those required for Verbal Reasoning, however there is a greater emphasis on **logical reasoning** rather than critical thinking, and **numerical skills** can be required for some questions, with a simple on-screen calculator provided for the duration of the section. As with Verbal Reasoning, you must be careful to avoid using your own knowledge to answer any of the questions, especially since certain question types present you with abstract scenarios and rules that do not reflect the real world.

As a doctor, you will often be required to make difficult decisions in complex and time-pressured scenarios. The variety of questions you can come across in this section reflects the enormous variety of situations you could be faced with as a medical professional. Whilst the time constraints aren't as tough here as they are in other sections of the UCAT, there is still a timer ticking down and a entire set of questions to answer. Therefore this section requires **high-level problem solving skills** and the ability to **assess risk and manage uncertainty.**

In the Decision Making section, you will be presented with 29 questions which can involve charts, text, tables, graphs, or diagrams. Much like Verbal Reasoning, there are two question formats. The first type asks you to respond to five statements, where you need to select *Yes* or *No* next to each statement. The second type takes a more traditional format, giving you four answer options with one being correct. You will come across a balance of these questions, so it is important you understand the various techniques you can use to tackle them in an efficient manner.

Within these question formats, three basic skills are assessed. The first of these is logical reasoning. This has been introduced in the Verbal Reasoning section of the guide, however we will further elaborate on different aspects of this broad skill that are most useful for Decision Making in this chapter, namely **interpreting information** and **drawing conclusions from a text,** as well as **probabilistic reasoning.** Also encompassed within this subdivision are **logical puzzles** where you must infer information based on a series of abstract statements. The next skill, **statistical reasoning,** is related to this, however the information that must be analysed comes in the form of graphs, tables, or even Venn diagrams. Finally, there are also quite a few questions that require you to assess a set of arguments and select the strongest one. This involves recognising assumptions within weak arguments and employing analytical skills to find the most logical and substantiated argument.

2.2 Core skills

2.2.1 Logical reasoning

Before diving into how logical reasoning is the cornerstone of the Decision Making section of the UCAT, we recommend you read the outline of logical reasoning in the Verbal Reasoning section of this guide on page 4. Here, we explained a number of important concepts such as deductive, inductive, and abductive reasoning. While knowledge of these terms is helpful for Verbal Reasoning, these concepts ultimately all combine in the form of recognising the difference between correlation and causation. In Decision Making, logical reasoning itself plays a huge role, and mastering its various forms can be very helpful in answering the array of questions that could be thrown at you.

The first kind of logical question you will encounter in this section of the UCAT is known as a syllogism. A **syllogism** is a type of logical argument that employs **deductive reasoning** to arrive at a conclusion using **at least two pieces of pieces of evidence or propositions.** The example of a deductive reasoning argument given in the Verbal Reasoning section of this guide is in fact a syllogism, and is restated below:

All people are mortal.
Socrates is a person.
Therefore, Socrates is a mortal.

In the context of Decision Making, you would be given the first two statements in the question stem and be required to deduce that the third statement follows. One of the tricky aspects of these questions is that the information provided may not necessarily make sense. Here is an example of a question stem that might perplex you:

All vehicles are either trucks or cars. All trucks are smaller than cars.

Clearly in real life, there are many different kinds of vehicles that exist and are not cars or trucks, and trucks are almost always bigger than cars. The issue is that regardless of what you know about the statements provided, you must assume that they are true are adapt your thought process to override these assumptions, allowing you to focus more on deductive reasoning, which is what this question type is really assessing.

Thus, as with Verbal Reasoning, you must **avoid bringing in any external knowledge** and make sure to read the question at least a few times to make sure you have a solid understanding of the 'rules' in the alternate reality created by the question. When reading the question, you should pay special attention to words describing how objects in the question relate to each other such as 'all,' 'no,' and 'some,' as these define the nature of the alternate reality.

One particularly helpful strategy you can use to tackle syllogism questions in the Decision Making section of the UCAT is to convert the statements in the question stem into a **Venn diagram.** This is not always possible or recommended, however in many cases it greatly simplifies the problem by allowing you to visualise the implications of the rules. Later on in this section, we will go into detail on how to interpret Venn diagrams as they are a common medium in which data you must analyse is presented in Decision Making questions, but for now we will just discuss how you can use Venn diagrams for syllogisms.

Syllogism Venn diagrams

For the purposes of explaining how to convert a syllogism into a Venn diagram, let's use the example of cars. Using this example, the first basic statement we may be presented with is:

Some cars are trucks.

If we convert this to a Venn diagram, the result is:

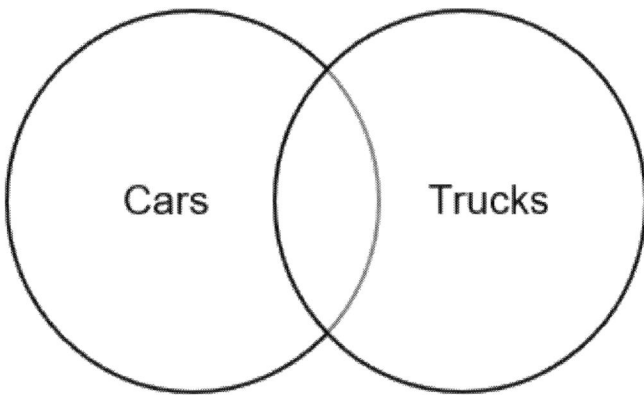

It may seem unnecessary to visualise this statement given its relative simplicity; however, when you are given multiple linked premises, it greatly reduces the number of opportunities there are for error.

To demonstrate how this Venn diagram could be helpful, imagine one of the conclusions they give you is:

Some cars are not trucks.

Again, the example statement is simple enough that you should be able to infer whether this is correct through mental deduction, however we will show the relevant region shaded, which proves that this conclusion is in fact true:

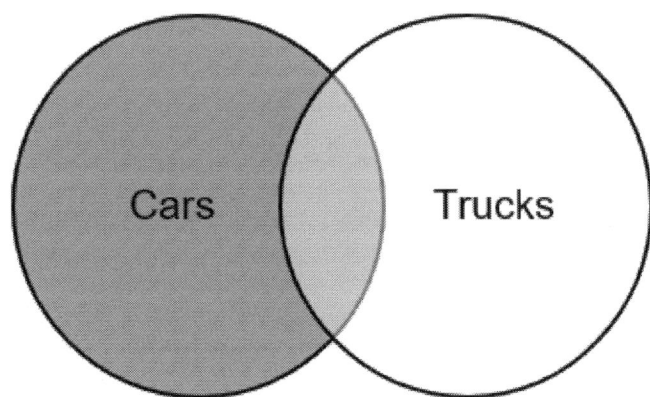

2.2 Core skills

There are two more basic situations you will be presented with that you must also add to your toolkit which you can use to create more complex Venn diagrams. The following examples will outline these before we move onto higher-order problem solving using Venn diagrams:

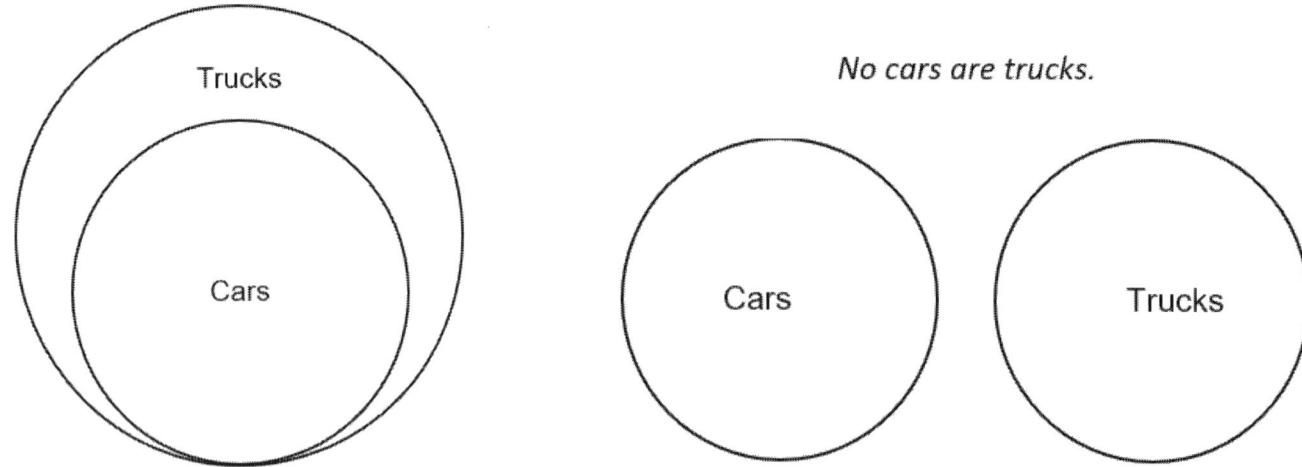

All cars are trucks.

No cars are trucks.

As mentioned previously, Venn diagrams really start to become useful when you are given multiple linked premises and several conclusions which you must validate. In these scenarios, spending time working through them with mental deduction will only confuse you and waste time. Let's now go through an example of a question stem you might find in the Decision Making section of the UCAT:

All cats are tigers. No cats are carnivores.

Before we proceed to looking at an example of a conclusion that could be given, it is important to visualise the problem with a Venn diagram.

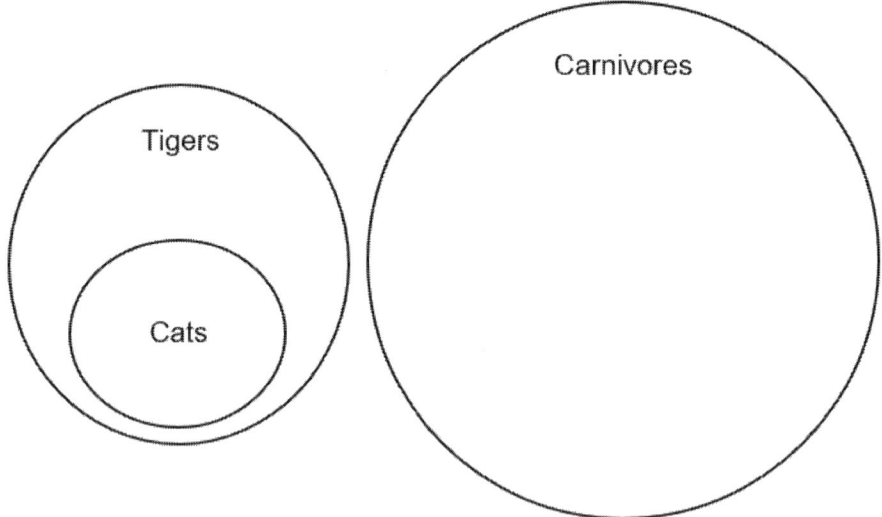

Here is an example of a conclusion you would need to assess if this was a question on the UCAT:

Some tigers are not carnivores.

The difficult aspect of this situation is that there is not much we can logically deduce about the relationship between tigers and carnivores. With that being said, we know that some tigers are cats, and that no cats are carnivores, so therefore we can say that some tigers are not carnivores, and thus the conclusion is correct. On the Venn diagram, we can visualise this as the separation between cats (which are clearly defined as a subset of tigers) and carnivores.

One important thing to note about syllogisms is that if there is **any uncertainty** surrounding the conclusion presented to you, then **you must assume that it is incorrect.** Using the previous example, you could be given a conclusion like this:

Some tigers are carnivores.

While there is a possibility that some tigers *could be* carnivores, we don't have enough information that the conclusion is completely correct, so you must assume it is incorrect as there is no evidence in the question stem to support it.

Now that we have covered syllogisms – an undoubtedly important part of Decision Making in the UCAT – let's talk about **interpreting information** from a text. Just like Verbal Reasoning, this section requires you to analyse material presented in a written format, and it is vital to keep your Verbal Reasoning skills and tricks in mind when completing these questions. However, using statistical reasoning is a much more important skillset for Decision Making, so you can go back to page 4 if you want to revise critical thinking and logical reasoning skills.

Probability questions

The next important skill required for the Decision Making section of the UCAT is **probabilistic reasoning.** As it is a form of deduction using maths, this falls under the category of logical reasoning. This is one of the few aspects of the UCAT that explicitly requires knowledge you have gained from high school. With that being said, you shouldn't be too worried about studying harder maths subjects as the probability knowledge required is quite basic and you should have covered it prior to your A-Levels studies. These questions are definitely some of the simpler ones you will find in this section, so you should make sure you are confident in **converting between fractions and percentages.** This will make it easy for you quickly complete these types of questions so you have extra time to spend on the more difficult ones.

One of the slight difficulties with this question type is that the answer is always either **Yes or No** depending on the question stem, however there are **four options** to choose from. Two of the options are Yes and two are No, each with **different associated reasoning.** This means that you must always be rigorous with your working out so you arrive at the correct answer via the most logical and correct method. Surprisingly, this can be helpful if you are running low on time. Often you can find **inconsistencies** in the reasoning provided in the answers, as they may either **contradict themselves or the information provided** in the question. Thus, you may be able to eliminate at least one or two options, greatly increasing your chances of selecting the correct answer if you need to make an educated guess.

Here is a quick example of a probability question you might find in the Decision Making section:

> **SAMPLE :**
> 4% of the cars that are sold from Dealership X are non-functional. Dealership Y also sells cars, with 90% of them being functional. On any given day, cars from Dealership X have a 1 in 8 chance of breaking down. Cars from Dealership Y have a 1 in 20 chance of breaking down on any given day.
>
> Based on functionality and chance of breaking down, which Dealership is the best to a buy car from?

There are a lot of numbers in this question, but the key is to simplify them down into one number for each Dealership, so we can easily compare which is the best one. The most logical approach is to multiply the probability of functionality with the chance of breaking down for each Dealership.

$$\text{Chance of car working} = \text{Probability of functionality} \times \text{Chance of not breaking down}$$

$$\text{Chance of car from dealership X working} = (1 - 0.04) \times \left(1 - \frac{1}{8}\right) = 0.84$$

$$\text{Chance of car from dealership Y working} = 0.9 \times \left(1 - \frac{1}{20}\right) = 0.855$$

After forming the necessary equation and performing the calculation for each Dealership, you can find that Dealership Y is slightly better at producing working cars.

Shape equations

As you may begin to realise, there are a lot of different skills involved in tackling the Decision Making section of the UCAT. Another skill that will come in handy is being able to deal with **shape equations.** This question type is not exceedingly common within the UCAT, but you will be presented with them at some stage, and you must be prepared so you can get as many marks as possible. Again, the main technique for answering these questions is covered in high school mathematics, namely applying the method of substitution to solve. I will provide a basic of example of what you can expect in the UCAT to demonstrate this method:

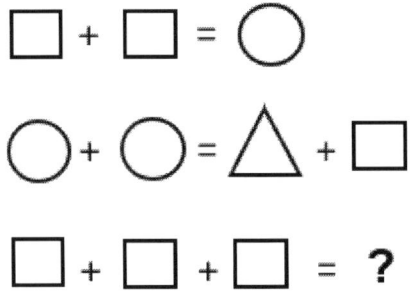

The first step is to substitute pronumerals for the shapes. Therefore, we could write the first equation in pronumerals as $2s = c$, where c = circle and s = square. In a similar vein, we can write the second equation as $2c = t + s$, where t = triangle. Substituting $c = 2s$, we can rewrite the second equation in terms of t and s as $4s = t + s$. We can simplify this into $t = 3s$. Conveniently, the question mark is equal to three squares in the third equation, so therefore we can conclude that the unknown variable is a triangle.

Obviously that example is quite simple, but the principles remain the same, so you should be able to quickly create some variables and scribble down some working out to solve any shape equation questions thrown at you during Decision Making. If you are having trouble understanding this, it may be worth reviewing high school algebra, which will also assist in the probabilistic reasoning we have already covered.

Logical puzzles

Now that I have covered the majority of the question types involving logical reasoning skills within the Decision Making section of the UCAT, it is time to discuss what is arguably its most difficult aspect. While all the previously discussed types of questions have robust strategies you can use to obtain the correct answer in a timely fashion, logical puzzles require **higher-order problem solving skills** and exhibit a **large amount of variety in question content.** In order to gain further insight into how to approach these questions, we must break down the term 'logical puzzle.' The word 'logical' implies that we should rigorously employ deductive inferences to verify which answer is correct. Again, this builds on the skills outlined in the Verbal Reasoning section of this guide. One important tool at your disposal is the ability to create a diagram. While this cannot be as specific as Venn diagrams for syllogisms, you should always try to find some logical way to visualise your thought process. Now onto the word 'puzzle' – this has connotations of trying to solve a complex problem that the creator has imbued with tricks and traps to make life more difficult for the solver. This is quite a common misconception as the UCAT question creators are really not trying to deceive you. In general, logical puzzles can present paths where you may get stuck, but through applying logical problem solving skills and carefully analysing the data you are presented with, the path to the answer should be clear. If you go in with a positive mindset that every question and puzzle is there to be solved, you will be more likely to find a way to answer them correctly. We will go through an example of how to tackle complex logical puzzles on page 32 to complete your understanding.

2.2.2 Statistical reasoning

Statistical reasoning can be considered a part of logical reasoning, but deserves its own section as there are some different skills required and the content of the questions moves away from blocks of text towards **tables and diagrams.** It is useful to have the information already visualised for you, however this means that you are usually required to make **inductive** rather than deductive inferences. In short, the data you are given are essentially conclusions, which you must use to **infer a rule or cause for the trend.** Some of the questions may be fairly simple, requiring you to analyse the data and make a prediction, but it can become more complex. If the question asks you to identify a cause and effect relationship within the data, you have to be very careful. As mentioned in the Verbal Reasoning section of this guide, **correlation does not equate to causation!** You should always be conservative in suggesting a causal relationship, even if it is supported by data. You must always look for a **temporal relationship,** where a cause directly precedes an effect, to check if you can assume there is causation.

As with many parts of the UCAT, you should avoid looking at any information before scanning through the questions. The data set they will provide you with will have too much information to process, so it is a waste of time to try and understand it before you look at what the question is asking of you. If you go straight to the questions, you will be able to save time as you will know which areas of the data to target for your analysis, and you can immediately cut out any superfluous information.

Now we have covered the general principles of statistical reasoning, we can look at a common and more specialised way that Decision Making questions assess this skill. There are a multitude of ways that you can visualise data, but using Venn diagrams is always one of the most favoured. Don't be fooled by the name though, as most of these Venn diagrams don't actually resemble the more traditional depiction, usually taking the form of various overlapping shapes that contain numbers to indicate the number of 'objects' in each subset. One of the tricky aspects of Venn diagram questions in the Decision Making section of the UCAT is that there are **two questions types.** Sometimes you will be provided with a Venn diagram and be required to select which statement matches it. In other situations, you must use a passage of information to determine which Venn diagram is correct.

Questions that provide a Venn diagram for you to use are the more simple form. You should be able to work through each of the answers and eliminate them if they are incorrect until you find an answer that fits the Venn diagram. In the case where you are required to select the Venn diagram based on a passage of text, you should ignore the answers when you start the question, and create your own Venn diagram from the information provided. When you are doing this, it is easiest to begin from the centre and incorporate information about all the categories in the Venn diagram first, before you move outwards. Once you are done, you should be able to match your own Venn diagram to one of the answers.

It is also important to recognise that there are some Venn diagram questions that do not involve Venn diagrams in the question stem or answer. These are known as **implied Venn diagram questions,** and can be recognised as they will list several 'objects' that fall into various categories and the question will ask you to find how many 'objects' are in a certain category. For these questions, it is essential that you construct your own Venn diagram as there is no other method for efficient solving. Let's look at a basic example to demonstrate how these questions are constructed.

> **SAMPLE:**
> From a survey of 100 science students, the following results were obtained:
> - 40 students study Physics
> - 37 students study Biology
> - 15 students study Physics and Chemistry
> - 13 students study Physics and Biology
> - 9 students study Chemistry and Biology
> - 8 students study Physics, Chemistry, and Biology

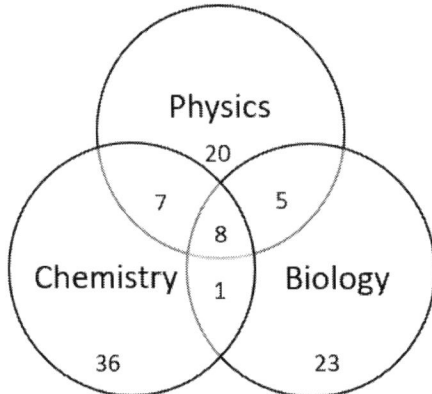

Here you can see the completed Venn diagram. Now that every section is complete, you would be able to use it to answer any question about categorical relationships. When you are making your own Venn diagrams for this question type, you should always keep the actual question in mind as you may be able to work out the necessary information without completing the entire Venn diagram, saving precious time. You must also always be careful when calculating the **intersection** between two of the three categories as you need to subtract the intersection between all of the three categories. Note that the question said 15 students study Physics and Chemistry, but we have put the number 7 in the corresponding section of the Venn diagram, as that number represents the students that study *only* Physics and Chemistry (i.e. not including the 8 that also study Biology). This further highlights the importance of **starting from the middle** of the Venn diagram and making sure to consider information pertaining to all categories first.

2.2.3 Evaluating arguments

Evaluating arguments is the final skill required to tackle the Decision Making section of the UCAT. It may feel a bit out of place as the questions are so subjective while the rest of Decision Making places an emphasis on logical reasoning and mathematical skills, however this is something of an illusion. These questions aren't looking for your opinion or analysis of an issue, they are **assessing your objectivity.** In many ways this is quite similar to how Verbal Reasoning targets critical thinking skills and how you must always establish a clear thought process free from bias and personal opinion.

In terms of how these questions are structured, you will be presented with a simple question that appears to ask for your opinion. You will then choose between four answer options:

1. **Yes,** for **Reason A.**
2. **No,** for **Reason B.**
3. **Yes,** for **Reason C.**
4. **No,** for **Reason D.**

The actual answer of Yes or No is quite irrelevant as the questions do not have any right or wrong answer, it just depends on your opinion. The key is that your select the **strongest argument of the four.** The first tip for approaching these questions is that you must be as objective as possible. The content of the questions may be provocative and make you feel a certain way that predisposes you to thinking the best answer is the one you agree with. However you have to set aside these feelings to select the strongest argument. This allows you to analyse each answer without being emotionally invested, so you can **explicitly target assumptions to rule out answers.**

Another piece of advice is to look for answers that are more **credible.** If an answer talks about how it has been proven or shown statistically, then there is a good chance that it is the strongest argument as it is backed by evidence. Conversely, if the answer mentions an opinion, then it is likely a weaker argument. We'll go through some examples of these questions on pages 31 and 33.

2.3 General advice for Section 2

2.3.1 How to prepare

Given the number of specific question types present within the Decision Making section of the UCAT, your preparation should be centred around **mastering each skill** before moving on to generalised practice with a focus on timing. You should initially go through the potential strategies you can use to tackle each type of question, keeping an open mind as some methods may be more useful than they appear. It is then best to start working through a few practice questions for each subsection of Decision Making to refine your technique. Since timing is not as much of an issue, you can spend longer on this phase of preparation, so you feel as comfortable as possible answering every permutation of question you can find in this section.

Before moving onto full practice exams, you should do a few timed Decision Making practice tests to get a feel for the pace. As stated in the Verbal Reasoning section, it is vital to spend more time **reviewing** the questions you have done rather than doing endless questions without any review, as analysing solutions for questions you got right and wrong will help you learn more, and enable you to improve your weaknesses.

It is important to also recognise the **passive benefits** of practising questions. Not only will you work out which strategies you want to employ for each question type, but you will also develop essential skills in critical thinking and logical reasoning. Following a logical thought process and recognising assumptions are vital to most Decision Making questions, and also provide significant benefits in other sections of the UCAT, yet they are difficult to master in their own right. Improving your abilities requires constant **self-reflection,** which is conveniently a by-product of practising questions and analysing your mistakes. When you are reviewing any practice questions, you should always think about the core skills you used to answer each particular question. Try to work through your thought process and figure out where your mistakes come from, or if there are any areas where you can save time.

Something else to also bear in mind is that many of the skills involved in Decision Making questions are also present in other sections. Questions involving **evaluating arguments** are quite similar to Verbal Reasoning critical thinking questions, while **mathematical questions** use virtually identical skills to what you will find in the Quantitative Reasoning section. This means that spending time preparing for these sections will also help with your Decision Making preparation, so it could be beneficial to streamline your approach by reducing your amount of targeted preparation for this section. However, you still need to make time for working out your strategy and doing some practice questions for this section too!

2.3.2 Tips for staying on time

With 31 minutes to complete 29 questions, Decision Making may appear to be a section where you don't have to worry too much about time. Unfortunately, for every question, you will need to process and decipher a large amount of information or data, often presented in a complex manner. While for Verbal Reasoning, every question stem has four associated questions, in Decision Making there is only one question, and the question may even come in five parts. This greatly increases your workload within the time limit, so you must have strategies ready to ensure you stay on time.

One of the most important things to do is to become proficient in using the tools provided. In terms of on-screen tools, a **virtual calculator** is provided in this section, and must be used for certain question types. Becoming familiar with using this should be part of your preparation, as it will certainly save you time and may also reduce your incidence of errors. You are also provided a **pen and booklet** to use for working out. Many Decision Making strategies rely on you creating your own visuals to understand information and data, so you need to be ready to quickly scribble down whatever is required to aid in your problem solving.

2.3.3 Running out of time

In the event that you do run out of time, it is advised that you completely change your general strategy rather than continue at the same rate and randomly guess the questions you haven't looked through by the very end. As with all sections of the UCAT, educated guesses are the key to success in dire situations, and there are quite of few question types you can target to increase your chances of making a correct guess in a very short amount of time.

With questions that ask you to make a conclusion based on information such as syllogisms and data interpretation, you can analyse the language and favour answers that have **soft or low modal language** such as the words 'may' or 'some,' as with Verbal Reasoning questions. Questions that ask you to analyse arguments can sometimes be guessed quickly if you look for answers that include some kind of substantiation such as a mention of statistics or expert opinion. Unfortunately, there are also some questions that are difficult to make educated guesses about. Logical puzzles, Venn diagrams, and probabilistic reasoning questions are structured in a way that makes them difficult to guess, so you should make a quick attempt and try to find a shortcut to the answer, or at least rule out one or two incorrect options before resorting to a random guess.

2.4 Strategy for *Yes and No* questions

As mentioned in the introduction to Decision Making, the first question format you will encounter for this section is a table with five statements relating to a question stem. It is your job to work through each of these statements and decide if the conclusion they draw follows from the information presented to you. If it does, then you select *Yes* as the answer, and if it doesn't, then you select *No* as the answer. In this section, we will outline some specific information about this question format, including some useful strategies for you to think about, before working through some examples to strengthen your understanding of the *Yes* and *No* questions along with the actual content of the Decision Making section of the UCAT.

2.4.1 Skills assessed by this question format

One of the unique aspects of Decision Making is that while there are two question formats, only certain question types can be assessed using each format. It is important to understand this information, as it can sometimes be exploited using knowledge of this scoring system, a topic that will be discussed below. One of the major types of questions exclusively tested through this question format is **interpretation of data in a graphical or written form.** Along with this, **syllogisms** are also assessed with five statements needing validation, which fully interrogate your skills in logical reasoning and problem solving. This means that for these question types, you must be prepared to gain a complete understanding of each problem as it is likely all aspects of the question stem will be covered by the five statements. In some cases, it may not be entirely detrimental to spend a bit more time looking at the information given to you prior to reading the statements you need to analyse, as it is likely most of the data you spend time understanding will be assessed in at least one of the five statements.

2.4.2 How scoring works

Scoring for *Yes* and *No* questions works quite differently to scoring for most other question formats in other sections of the UCAT. Usually, you are given one mark for a correct answer and no marks for an incorrect answer; however, with this question format, there are a **maximum of two marks** up for grabs. If you wish to obtain the full two marks, you must select the **correct option for all five statements.** One mark is awarded if your answer is **partially correct** (i.e. if you only get 4/5 statements correct). This is quite unforgiving as even one slip up can result in you losing half of your potential marks. Clearly this question format demands perfection, yet can yield high rewards if you are willing to spend a bit more time on it. Therefore, if you feel you have worked out the correct answer to all five statements, it can be worth investing some extra time in checking you haven't made any silly mistakes, as this small effort could earn you another mark. This is preferable to starting a new question that is only worth one mark and might be significantly more difficult than the one you are working on.

The following Decision Making example demonstrates how syllogisms are assessed through using five *Yes* and *No* statements.

> **SAMPLE:**
> *This image is a photo. All photos are coloured.*
>
> Before going through the example statements associated with this syllogism, we should create a Venn diagram to visualise the image, which will allow us to solve every statement far more quickly.
>
>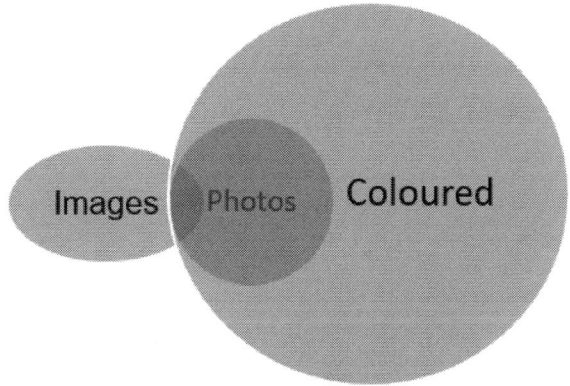
>
> - **Statement 1:** "All images are photos."
>   The statement "this image is a photo" implies that there is at least one image that is a photo, but there is no information to infer that all images are photos. This is reflected in the Venn diagram drawn to visualise the scenario, where we have illustrated the relationship that some images are photos. This is the only safe inference at this point. Thus, the answer is *No*.
> - **Statement 2:** "All images are coloured."
>   This statement follows on from the preceding one. We have already ascertained that there could be images that are not photos, and by the same logic there could images that are not coloured, as the only thing we do know is that "all photos are coloured". Thus, the answer is also *No*.
> - **Statement 3:** "Some photos are coloured."
>   This is a deceptively simple statement. Since we know from the information that "all photos are coloured," then we can conclude that some of those photos are coloured as they are simply a subset of "photos" bubble on the Venn diagram. Thus, the answer is *Yes*.
> - **Statement 4:** "All coloured photos are images."
>   This is where the statements tend to become trickier, as they involve more than two of the categories and often reverse the logic of the information. One thing to note is that the statement "coloured photos" is superfluous as we already know that all photos are coloured, further emphasising how these statements can sometimes be confusing. The key here is to remain calm and work through it in a logical manner. In this case, we can look back on the Venn diagram and see that there is an incomplete confirmed overlap between photos and images, so therefore the answer is *No*.
> - **Statement 5:** "Everything that is not an image is not coloured."
>   This final statement takes the goal of confusing test-takers even further by adding a double negative! You always have to be careful with these, as they can easily misdirect you. This statement deals with "everything that is not an image," which is a completely unknown section of the Venn diagram. Stating that this entire set is "not coloured" is an invalid inference as there is no information to suggest that the coloured section on the Venn diagram is a set exclusive to photos. Thus, the answer is *No*.

The next worked example highlights how you can efficiently interpret information from visuals such as graphs. Data analysis questions always come up in the Decision Making section of the UCAT, so it is vital you understand how to quickly gather specific information to answer every statement in the set correctly. Remember to gain a brief understanding of what the graph is trying to say, but avoid spending too much time as you need to swiftly move onto answering each statement.

2.4 Strategy for Yes and No questions

SAMPLE:
This graph depicts the number of cases of viral and bacterial respiratory infections reported over the course of the year in a certain location in the southern hemisphere.

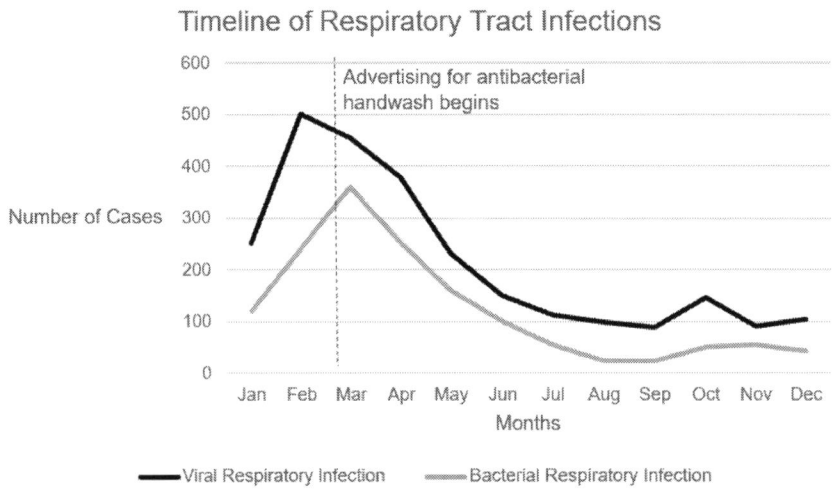

- **Statement 1:** "Viral respiratory infections are brought on by heat and sunshine."
There is very little correlation between the summer months and cases of viral respiratory tract infections. While the peak is in February, January and December of the same year do not demonstrate significant peaks compared to other time periods. Even if there was a strong correlation, there is no information to suggest that the summer in question was hot or had much sunshine. For all we know, it was one of the coolest and darkest summers of all time, so there are absolutely no grounds to assume this statement is correct. Thus, the answer is *No*.
- **Statement 2:** "The prevalence of bacterial respiratory infections was reduced by the March antibacterial handwash advertising campaign."
This is an issue of correlation and causation. While the prevalence of bacterial respiratory infections does decrease immediately after this campaign, we have to apply **abductive reasoning** and think about this. Would advertising for this handwash really have such a profound and immediate effect, or is there another more logical reason? In this case there is a more likely event that has triggered the reduction, which will be explained in response to the next statement. Thus, the answer is *No*.
- **Statement 3:** "The prevalence of bacterial respiratory infections mostly follows that of viral respiratory infections."
The correlation between viral and bacterial respiratory infections is the more likely explanation we hinted at when discussing Statement 2. Aside from having a logical link, there is the key criteria of a **temporal relationship.** A cause and effect relationship must have the cause shown to be happening distinctly before the effect, as with the reductions in viral and bacterial infections. Thus, the answer is *Yes*.
- **Statement 4:** "There was probably an increase in antibacterial handwash sales in January."
This statement is designed to trick you. You may automatically think that the advertising campaign should increase sales and waste time pondering whether this is a fair assumption, however this is completely irrelevant. You have to be careful as the statement says the potential increase was in January, which is illogical from a temporal standpoint as the assumed cause of this increase, the advertising campaign, occurred in March. Thus, the answer is *No*.
- **Statement 5:** "The cooler winter months increase the potency of bacteria of the respiratory tract."
This statement again provides no evidence-based assertions. We have no means of assessing whether the winter months were in fact cooler, and there is no increase in bacterial respiratory infections, so we can only assume that there is no change in potency over this time period. Thus, the answer is *No*.

2.5 Strategy for *Single Best Answer* questions

The second question format found in the Decision Making section of the UCAT is more traditional, providing a question stem with information and four answer options you must choose from. Like most questions in the UCAT, there is one mark available should you select the correct answer. Given that these questions are less valuable than *Yes* and *No* questions, you must be constantly aware of how much time you are spending on them. To save as much time as possible, you should only look at the information from the question stem with the purpose of checking whether one of the answer options is correct or incorrect. Using this strategy will leave you with more time to tackle the higher value question format, where investing more time will generally result in a greater reward.

2.5.1 Skills assessed by this question format

Single best answer questions are used to test all the other question types not mentioned in the corresponding section in the *Yes* and *No* question format strategy guide. This includes **probabilistic reasoning, shape equations, logical puzzles, Venn diagrams, and evaluating arguments.** For these question types, you must be prepared to **analyse four different answer options,** which can take some time, especially since they may be in a written or visual form. For probabilistic reasoning and evaluating arguments, you need to remember that along with an answer that is *Yes* or *No*, you must acknowledge the correct reasoning to pick the right answer.

The following example demonstrates how skills relating to evaluating arguments can be used to approach certain single best answer questions in the UCAT. You will find this type of question features prominently in the Decision Making section, and while it appears to be like a simpler Verbal Reasoning question, the overt testing of critical thinking skills can challenge you in many ways. It is important to remember that while the information in the question stem is posed as a question, the real question will always be asking for your **objective opinion on which argument is strongest.**

> SAMPLE :
>
> *"Should eSports feature in the Olympics?"*
>
> **Question: Select the strongest argument from the statements below.**
>
> - **Option 1:** "Yes, eSports are just as competitive and skilful as other, more physically involved Olympic sports."
>   When evaluating this argument, we must ignore whether it agrees or disagrees with the question, and also let go of our biases, as they will only cloud our objective judgement. In regards to the argument in question, it is not as strong as we would like due to the fact that it is simply an opinion. There is no substantiation of the claim that eSports are similar in skill and competition to other Olympic sports, and thus it is unlikely that this is the correct option. Of course, we cannot rule it out at this stage, but once you have looked through each option, you should be able to make an informed judgement.
> - **Option 2:** "Yes, statistics from the most recent Olympics show there was a 30% drop in viewers from the 18–34 age group, and the addition of eSports could renew interest from younger demographics."
>   This argument is more promising as it is a statement that is supported by statistics and makes a good point that the Olympics needs to appeal to younger fans in order to survive. It is also strong as it does not directly compare eSports and Olympics in subjective terms. At this stage, you would certainly be favouring this as the correct answer, but you should always read through all the options before you choose.
> - **Option 3:** "No, less physically involved but highly respected games like chess are not Olympic sports, and therefore eSports do not deserve to be Olympic sports."
>   Comparing eSports to chess is not the strongest argument as you cannot equate the two completely different games and then use this to prove something. The word "deserve" also shows that the entire statement is an unsubstantiated opinion, and thus this is not the correct answer, especially when you compare it to the preceding option.

2.5 Strategy for Single Best Answer questions

> - **Option 4:** "No, eSports cannot be considered real sports as there is no physical skill involved." This is not a completely invalid argument, but it is clearly outclassed by Option 2, which involves statistics and prevents a clearly unbiased argument. From what we can see in this argument, it is most certainly an opinion, and the words "real sport" hint that the argument is founded on a belief that Olympic sports are inherently better than eSports, and fails to present a compelling reason.

The following question is an example of a logical puzzle. There will be at least a few of these in the Decision Making section of the UCAT, and they are quite difficult as they require problem solving skills using different variable sets. The key here is to keep track of all the combinations without getting overwhelmed, so you can fully analyse the problem.

> **SAMPLE:**
> There are five students who receive their school grades at the end of the year. Their names are Zang, Ning, Gary, Rolt, and Fatima. In no particular order:
>
> - Their Geography marks are 68, 74, 77, 79, 81, and 83.
> - Their History marks are 55, 63, 75, 76, and 88.
> - Their English marks are 60, 66, 73, 75, 79, and 82.
>
> Additionally:
>
> - The person with an English mark of 79 has a History mark that is one mark higher than Zang's.
> - Gary has the highest Geography mark and has a History mark of 63.
> - Rolt has an English mark that is 19 more than Fatima.
> - The person with the highest History mark has the lowest English mark.
>
> **Question: What is Ning's History mark?**

Instead of going through each potential option for this question, we will work through how to visualise all the data and logically deduce the answer. For this question type, the options generally aren't worth looking at as they won't give you any hints. In this specific example, there is a lot of data to digest so we need to create a table to keep track of the known information.

	Zang	Ning	Gary	Rolt	Fatima
Geography mark			83		
History mark	75		63	76	88
English mark				79	60

Starting with the first statement, we can ascertain that Zang has a History mark of 75, as there is only one set of History marks with a one mark gap between them. For the second piece of information, we can simply insert Gary's marks for those two subjects into the table with no inference needed. We can use a similar technique for the third statement as we did for the first statement to infer Rolt and Fatima's English marks. Now we know who has the English mark of 79, we can go back to the first statement and work out that Rolt must have a History mark of 76. We can also now use the fourth piece of information to conclude that Fatima has a History mark of 88. Now we have finally used all the information from the statements, there is only one more deduction required to obtain the information to answer the question. Now we know 4 out of 5 of the History marks, we can work out that Ning's History mark must be 55.

That concludes the Decision Making section of this guide. Decision Making questions test a variety of skills, even dabbling in mathematical and text analysis, making it something of a fusion between Verbal Reasoning and Quantitative Reasoning, the next section of this guide. We hope you will find some of strategies within this section useful and use them to succeed in Decision Making. There are a further two sample questions after this for you to gain a greater understanding of the structure of Decision Making questions and how to apply different techniques for solving. Good luck!

2.6 Sample questions

SAMPLE:

Either Bob or John won the 100 m sprint. All participants in the sprint were Year 12 students except for Bob. Some of these sprinters also participated in the high jump. Furthermore, no student from Year 11 won the 100 m sprint.

Select **Yes** if the conclusion follows. Select **No** if the conclusion does not follow.

1.	"John is a Year 12 student, so he participated in the high jump."	Yes / No
2.	"Bob won the 100 m sprint, and John is a Year 11 student."	Yes / No
3.	"Bob is not a Year 12 student, so he did not participate in the high jump."	Yes / No
4.	"If a Year 12 student won the 100m sprint, then Bob must be a Year 11 student."	Yes / No
5.	"The sprinters who participated in the high jump were Year 12 students."	Yes / No

SAMPLE:

In order to reduce rates of diabetes mellitus type 2, should there be a tax on sugar?

Question: Select the strongest argument from the statements below.

(a) Yes, excessive sugar consumption is a direct cause of diabetes mellitus type 2, which is a substantial burden on healthcare system.
(b) Yes, it could dissuade children from eating too much sugar, causing them to be less hyperactive and not as annoying.
(c) No, the public should be free to purchase whatever goods they like at a fair price.
(d) No, this could reduce the number of customers at stores dependent on selling sugary food, causing unemployment.

2.7 Answers to sample questions

Question 1: No

We know that John was in the 100 m sprint, and that all sprinters were Year 12 students except Bob, so it is safe to assume that John is a Year 12 student. The second part of the statement is where we run into trouble, as we cannot infer that he participated in the high jump since only some of the sprinters did the high jump, and there is no specific information to suggest he is in the group.

Question 2: No

This statement must be false as we have already ascertained that John is a Year 12 student, as all sprinters except Bob are in Year 12.

Question 3: No

The information in the question stem tells us that Bob is not a Year 12 student, but this does not prohibit him from participating in the high jump, as we know that some of the sprinters did participate, and there is no information to suggest he was prohibited due to the fact that he was not a Year 12 student.

Question 4: No

The issue with this statement is that there is no information specifying Bob's actual year level, as he could very well be in Year 10 or below for all we know.

Question 5: No

Again, this statement does not account for the fact that Bob is not a Year 12, and can also participate in the high jump as he is a sprinter.

Question 6: A

Option A is the best option as it involves a very logical argument with a compelling conclusion that focuses on widespread implications of the tax. Options B and C are clearly very opinionated and offer no statistics to improve the value of their arguments. Option D has a strong conclusion that focuses on an important factor of unemployment, however the logic of its argument is somewhat murky, as we don't know if the potential reduction would be enough to significantly affect unemployment levels.

Section 3

Section 3 – Quantitative Reasoning

3.1 Introduction

The third section of the UCAT is Quantitative Reasoning, and as the name suggests, it is entirely focused on **mathematics.** Candidates will receive 1 minute to read instructions and 24 minutes for the test itself. In terms of content, all questions involve **numerical skills** and assume you have covered **basic mathematical concepts** during high school. It is important to note, however, that the questions are *not* designed to test how good you are at maths. They simply use maths to assess your **problem solving skills within clearly defined limits,** given that mathematics is rigorously based around a set of rules.

Quantitative Reasoning is a section of UCAT because doctors must be familiar with using numbers in a variety of ways. On a basic level, you need to be able to quickly calculate and utilise numbers relating to patient details such as age and weight along with other quantitative factors. In terms of more advanced skills, clinical research involves analysing and presenting data in complex ways, so you must be comfortable with interpreting numerical information.

In this section, you will be presented with **36 questions** along with their associated data or visuals. You will have **five options** to choose from for each question, meaning that educated guesses are a lot more difficult, and random guesses will have a much lower return. Much like Verbal Reasoning, there is a significant time pressure in this section, so adequate preparation is essential to become familiar with the various data presentations and questions formats.

Most questions you will find in Quantitative Reasoning come in **sets of four** and are based off the same question stem, thus testing that you have a complete understanding of all aspects of the data and requiring a thorough process of reasoning. There are still some standalone questions, but it is imperative that you streamline your approach to these as much as possible so you have more time for the associated question sets, where more marks are available. As with Decision Making, an **on-screen calculator** is provided, however you will be required to use it much more, so familiarity is essential to increase your pace.

In terms of question types, you will face a variety of challenges requiring different mathematical skills to apply to solve the problems. This includes **basic arithmetic, proportionality, ratios, percentages, finances, geometry, statistics, and physics conversions** involving speed, distance, and time. We will cover the most important of these skills in more detail in the following section, so you understand exactly how these are assessed in the Quantitative Reasoning section of the UCAT, and what you need to know to successfully tackle them.

3.2 Core skills

3.2.1 Ratios

A ratio is a **comparison of the amount of one thing relative to another thing.** Rather than being an absolute measure such as weight or height, a ratio divides a total number of items into parts for easy comparisons. When dealing with ratios, you must always remember that **whole numbers** should be used and the ratio should be expressed in the **simplest form.** This process is usually not too complicated as you just need to find a factor to either increase or decrease the ratio depending on the specifications.

For example, if you have the ratio 10:4, you need to reduce it to 5:2 in order to find the correct answer. If there is a decimal in your ratio such as in the example of 1.5:4, you must express it as 3:8. You should make sure to practise being vigilant in this regard, as failure to simplify ratios is a fairly costly error. It can also be frustrating as it is not generally what the question is trying to assess, but it's still something you need to take care to get right. Sometimes you can use estimation to quickly find a simple ratio when the question doesn't require an exact answer. This situation doesn't occur very often, but it is important to bear in mind as you can save a lot of time.

3.2 Core skills

Now we have covered the basic principles of ratios, we can look at specific scenarios in the UCAT where you can find ratios. Here is an example of one of the simpler ratio questions you can find in the Quantitative Reasoning section of the UCAT.

> **SAMPLE :**
> *There are 52 students in a year level. They all play one sport according to the ratio 3:5:1:4 which corresponds to kayaking, cricket, softball, and tennis respectively.*
>
> **Question: How many students play cricket?**

This question gives you the total number and ratio, so the first thing you need to do is add up the total number of parts in this ratio. In this case, there are 13 parts in the ratio (3+5+1+4). If you divide 52 by 13, you get 4, so now we have a factor we can use to compare the relative ratio to the absolute number of students. To finish the problem, we just have to multiply this factor by the numbers of parts in the ratio that corresponds to cricket. Performing this calculation (4×5) yields 20. So therefore, the answer to the question is that 20 students play cricket. As you can see with this question, you need a strong understanding of how to link ratios with the values assigned to them using basic arithmetic, so if you are struggling, it could be useful to review some chapters from your high school mathematics textbook.

With ratios being a substantial element of Quantitative Reasoning, it's time to explore the complex aspects of this question type, namely how it can be used in conjunction with **units on maps.** This can often be extended into **area questions,** where the information is presented in a less accessible format. Obviously, this means you must be very comfortable converting distances from millimetres all the way to kilometres. This can be tricky for many students as it is easy to become confused and waste time wondering whether to divide or multiply, and by what factor of 10. Before diving into examples, we will first go through the process of converting distances and areas. It is highly recommended that you memorise this information as you may become flustered during the test and you should have a strong knowledge base to refer to.

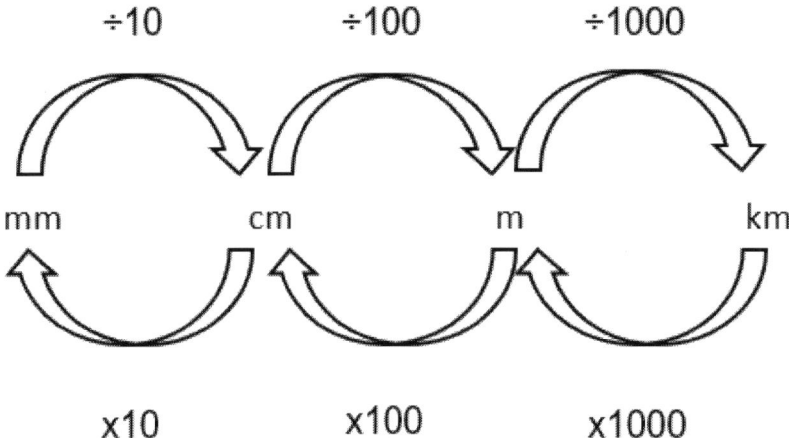

Now that we have refreshed your knowledge of distance conversions, let's go through an example of how this type of question can appear in the UCAT.

> **SAMPLE :**
> *A group of travellers are looking at a map of Oakfield and find that the scale of the map is 1:14000. The distance between the Oak Hotel and the Lighthouse is measured on the map and found to be 9 cm.*
>
> **Question: How many km is this in real life?**

The first thing to do when looking at this question is to recognise the unit conversion that must take place. From the question stem, we know we are working with distances and must convert cm to km. Using the scale of the map and a calculator, we can multiply 9 × 14000 to work out that the distance between the Oak Hotel and the Lighthouse is 126,000 cm. To find the answer, we just need to convert this into m and then into km. Dividing by 100 makes the distance 1,260m and finally dividing by 1,000 gives us 1.26 km.

Another kind of map question you can find that involves unit conversions is the area question. With **area conversions,** there is the added trick of having to **square each factor** when you are jumping between units, as areas are measured in units^2. This can often be avoided, however; and if you get the chance, you should always convert all distances into the desired units before do the final area calculation. To demonstrate this technique, let's look at a continuation of the previous example.

> SAMPLE :
> A group of travellers are looking at a map of Oakfield and find that the scale of the map is 1:14000. On the map, the Oakfield Recreation Centre has a length of 3 cm and width of 8 cm.
>
> **Question: What is the area of this building in km in real life?**

As this question relates to the previous example, we can jump straight in and begin converting each dimension of the building before the final area calculation. Multiplying 3 × 14000 gives 42,000 cm, and this can be converted into 0.42 km through the same process as with the last example. Multiplying 8 × 14000 results in 112,000 cm, which is 1.12km. Now the conversion is done, it's time to calculate the area by multiplying the dimensions. 0.42 × 1.12 gives us an answer of 0.4704 km^2 as the area. This is the ideal process for working through area questions, as doing the individual conversions allows you to avoid the tricky method of converting areas using the squared factors.

3.2.2 Percentages

A large number of questions in the Quantitative Reasoning section of the UCAT use percentages or fractions, and you are expected to be familiar enough with them to quickly convert between them or use them for calculations. As with ratios, a percentage is an expression of a number of parts from a total; however, it is a more dynamic measure and is generally out of 100. One of the key skills required to approach this question type is the ability to quickly **inflate or reduce** a given number by a set percentage. Consider the following example.

> SAMPLE :
> **Question:** *The price of a watch is £132. If it is on a 18% sale, how much does the watch cost?*

While this example is fairly simple, you will typically find this in a question set with a lot of other information in the question stem, so you should aim to complete this in at most 20 seconds. Doing the mental maths is not going to be fast enough as the numbers involved aren't going to give a nice result, but inputting all the steps of calculation into the on-screen calculator is also going to be time-consuming and clunky. The optimal method uses **both mental arithmetic and the calculator.** The first step is to swiftly find an easy equation to type into the calculator. The full equation to work this out is 132 × (1 − 0.18) but we can streamline this process by doing the subtraction in our head and putting 132 × 0.82 into the calculator. You can save further time by just putting in 132 × .82, as technically the zero is redundant and over the course of the section, exploiting these kinds of quick calculator tricks could give you a considerable amount of extra time. Using the calculator in this fashion yields the correct answer of £108.24.

Percentages are also used in problem solving questions where information is given to you in different forms and you must work your way to the answer. This type of question is not entirely dissimilar to logical puzzles in Decision Making, however it requires confidence in numerical reasoning and comfort in dealing with percentages and conversions. Let's now go through an example to demonstrate how you can use your skills in percentage changes to tackle these questions.

3.2 Core skills

> **SAMPLE :**
> Last week Lenny spent £150 on water and £90 on electricity. He also spent 33.33% of the cost of last week's water on food in the same week. His spending on water, electricity, and food constituted 40% of his expenses for the week.
>
> **Question: How much did Lenny spend in total last week?**

We are given the information that Lenny spent £150 on water and £90 on electricity so the first thing to do is work out Lenny's spending on food. This is simple enough as it is 33.33% of the £150 spent on water, which can be worked out in your head to be £50. Now we add these together so we can work out that 40% of his expenses equates to £290 (150+90+50). Now we know this value, all we need to do is divide £290 by 40% to work out the total spending. If you find yourself getting confused over whether to multiply or divide at this stage, remember that multiplying by a percentage (assuming it is <100) reduces the number and dividing increases the number, so you can use the context of the situation to figure the operator to utilise. Using the calculator efficiently, we can input 290 ÷ .4 to find the correct answer of £725.

3.2.3 Financial mathematics

Questions involving finances feature prominently in the Quantitative Reasoning section of the UCAT. More specifically, these questions focus on problem solving relating to **interest and tax.** Questions on interest fall under two categories, either focusing on simple interest or compound interest. With **simple interest**, you must remember that the amount earned is fixed over time. For example, if you saved £50 with a simple interest rate of 2% per annum then you would earn £1 each year. There is also a formula you can use to assist you with any problem solving questions:

$$\text{Simple interest} = \text{Principal} \times \text{Rate} \times \text{Time}$$

In this example, the original amount of £50 would be the principal and 2% p.a. ('per annum' or per year) would be the rate. If this were an actual UCAT question, the stem would also mention a length of time so you could complete the calculation to find the simple interest earned. **Compound interest** is where this becomes more complicated, as the interest earned is continually added to the principal, leading to an increased amount earned over time. For example, if you saved £50 with a compound interest rate of 20% per annum, then you would earn £10 in the first year, and £12 next year as the £10 earned from the first year is added to the principal to calculate the next year's interest. As with simple interest, you can use a formula help with your calculations:

$$\text{Compound interest} = \text{Principal} \times \left[(1 + \text{Rate per period})^{\text{Number of periods}} - 1\right]$$

If you are using this formula, you must remember that the amount of time is not an absolute measure, but really depends on the number of periods specified by the rate. For instance, if you are calculating compound interest that has a rate of 2% per 6 months over 4 years, then your amount of time is not 3 years, but 8 periods of time, as your principal will be added to every 6 months over the course of that time period.

Now that we've covered the basics of interest, we can look at how this type of question can be assessed in the UCAT, and what strategies you should employ.

> **SAMPLE:**
> Amy puts £7,000 into a bank account, which returns 6.5% p.a. on a variable amount year on year.
>
> **Question: By the start of the fourth year, how much will she have earned?**

The first thing to do is to work out whether the question is asking you to calculate simple or compound interest. This is sometimes not explicitly stated, so you must be vigilant. In this case, the fact that the returns are based on a **variable amount** each year indicates that you are dealing with **compound interest.** It is also important to note that the amount of time is 3 years, as the question states that we want to know the amount earned by the start of the fourth year, which does not include the fourth year. Now we have cleared up the ambiguities of the question, we can simply input the information into the formula. This means that the compound interest can be calculated by the equation $7000 \times [(1 + 0.065)^3 - 1]$, giving us the answer £1,455.65 to the nearest pence.

Along with questions on interest, there are also tax questions in the Quantitative Reasoning section of the UCAT, utilising similar skills with a bit more complexity. Most tax questions will give you a table in the question stem that looks something like this:

Annual taxable income bracket (£)	Tax rate	Total tax paid at the top of this taxable income bracket (£)
0 – 10,000	10%	1,000
10,000 – 25,000	15%	3,250
25,000 – 50,000	25%	9,500
50,000 and over	40%	

The confusing thing about tax brackets is that you cannot calculate tax as a flat rate, as someone who earns more than £10,000 will pay tax at **different rates for different sections of their money.** For instance, if you earn £35,000 then you will pay 10% tax on the first £10,000, 15% on the next £15,000 and 25% on the final £10,000. You can use the column on the right to quickly add up this amount as we know that you will have to pay £3,250 tax on your first £25,000 and then we just need to add 25% of the extra £10,000 you earn in the third tax bracket. This amounts to a total tax of £5,750. This type of quick tax calculation question is fairly common in this section of the UCAT, so it is important that you become familiar with **interpreting tax tables** and using the on-screen calculator efficiently, as the numbers they use to assess your skills won't be as friendly as the ones in this example.

As with most question types in Quantitative Reasoning, you will also need to apply your skills to tackle more difficult problem solving questions. While these are less common, it is still important to be able to complete them, and practising them will further solidify your technique.

This is an example of an application-style question, using the tax table from above.

> **SAMPLE:**
> **Question: Andrew pays £8,300 of income tax each year. What is his annual taxable income?**

This question is more difficult as we must work backwards using the tax to find taxable income. The first thing to do is to work out which tax bracket Andrew is in. As his annual income tax is £8,300, we know he is in the third tax bracket, which has income taxes ranging from £3,250 to £9,500, indicated in the third column of the tax table. Now we know he earns at least £25,000, we must find out what additional money he earns on top of that so we can add them together to find his total income.

This means we need to subtract the £3,250 tax he has accrued due to his income being at least £25,000, so we can find out how much he is taxed for his income exceeding £25,000. If we subtract £3,250 from £8,300 it leaves £5,050. We know from the tax table that £5,050 must be 25% of his additional income, so we can use our skills with percentages to find the suitable equation £5,050 ÷ 0.25, which gives us a result of £20,200. If we add this additional income to the £25,000 we had already taxed, then we can find the total taxable income to be £45,200.

As you can see, this more complex application question involves many of the skills we have already covered such as dealing with interest and percentages, demonstrating how understanding and practice can have compounding effects on improving your results.

3.2.4 Statistics

Questions relating to statistics play an important role in the Quantitative Reasoning section of the UCAT, so you must have a strong understanding of the core skills required to tackle this type of question. The concept of the **mean** is particularly vital to grasp, as this will be the focus of many statistical questions. The most basic element you can encounter is the **arithmetic mean,** which you should already understand as the regular average where all numbers in the set carry an equal weighting. This can easily be calculated by finding the sum of the data points and dividing by the number of items in the set. Given the relative simplicity of this, it is unlikely you will find any questions exploring this concept in the UCAT. Quantitative Reasoning instead tends to focus on the idea of the **weighted mean,** where numbers in the data set are weighted differently, allowing for more meaningful analysis. As with most things in maths, you can use a formula to calculate this:

$$\text{Weighted mean} = \sum(\text{Each number from the data set} \times \text{Individual weighting})$$

This formula isn't particularly useful in solving questions, but it nicely encapsulates the process you must go through the calculate the weighted mean. The symbol before the brackets represents the words 'sum of,' meaning that you must add together each product of the number and weighting until you have done it for every data point. The numerical skills involved in approaching this type of question are somewhat complex, so let's work through an example to demonstrate how to calculate the weighted mean.

SAMPLE :

The following table outlines Kate's results for Biology.

Assessment	Weighting (%)	Result (%)
Test	10	92
Assignment	15	77
Written exam	50	84
Practical exam	25	63

Question: Use this to calculate Katie's final mark as a percentage.

This example may be slightly more convenient than what you could find in the UCAT, as they will often hide weighted mean questions by not explicitly stating the weighting, so you must always be vigilant!

But since this information given to us, we can start out calculations. Rather than adding our set of numbers and dividing by 4 like we would do in an arithmetic mean question, we need to **multiply each result by its weighting** and then add them to find the final mark. It is important to note that the weightings are expressed as percentages, so we must convert them to decimals for the purposes of the calculation. This gives us the equation $(92 \times 0.1) + (77 \times 0.15) + (84 \times 0.5) + (63 \times 0.25)$, which gives the correct answer of 79%.

3.2.5 Physics

Physics forms a part of the Quantitative Reasoning section of the UCAT in the form of **speed, distance, and time questions,** which often involve accompanying graphs. If you are given any two of variables, you can always calculate the third variable, according the diagram below.

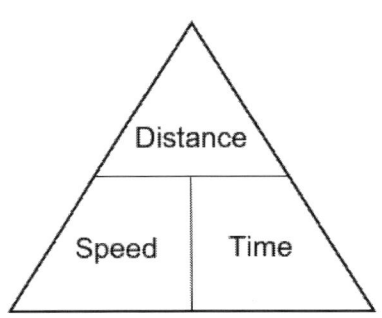

You can use this triangle to derive all the formulas required by ignoring or physically covering the unknown variable. If you need speed, you can see that distance is over time. If you need distance, you can see that speed is next to time, indicating multiplication. Finally, if you need time, it is distance over speed. Now we can write out these formulas for convenience, but you don't need to worry about memorising them as they can be derived from the diagram. It is important to note that the formulas only work if speed is in metres/second, distance is in metres and time is seconds, so conversions may be required depending on the content of the question.

$$\text{Speed} = \frac{\text{Distance}}{\text{Time}} \quad | \quad \text{Distance} = \text{Speed} \times \text{Time} \quad | \quad \text{Time} = \frac{\text{Distance}}{\text{Speed}}$$

When you are working through these kinds of questions, you will find that you need to use these formulas in conjunction with analysing distance-time or even velocity-time graphs. **Velocity** is essentially speed in a certain direction. Speed must always be positive, however velocity can be negative if something travels in the opposite direction. If you think about a car travelling in a certain direction at 40 km/h, you could say that its speed and velocity are both 40 km/h. If it then stops and starts reversing at 40 km/h, its speed is still 40 km/h, but it's velocity is −40 km/h. **Acceleration** also comes into play when looking at velocity-time graphs and is simply the gradient of a line (much like velocity is the gradient of the distance-time graph). If you feel confused by any of this, don't worry too much as if this does come up, it is likely the question stem will give you some assistance with formulas. For now, we will focus on an example of how to use speed, distance and time formulas in distance-time graph questions.

SAMPLE :
The graph shows the distance two cars are from a certain point at different times.

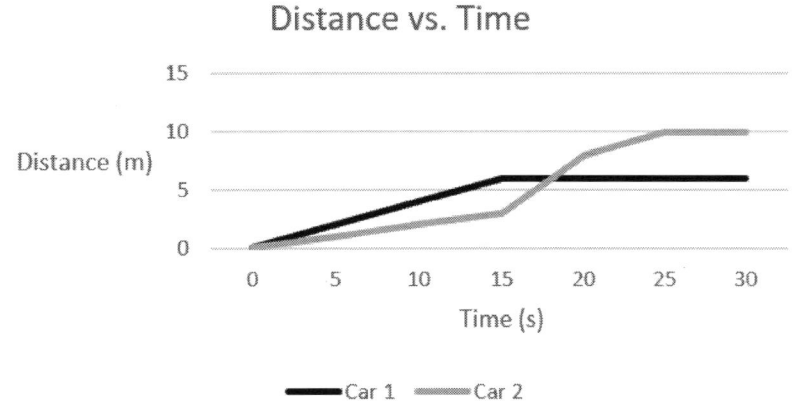

Question: What is the difference between the average speed of each car over the 30 second journey to two decimal places?

The best method to solve this question is to first use the graph to get the data points for each car and then use the equations to find the speed of each car across the journey, before finally subtracting the speed of Car 2 from Car 1 to find the difference. For Car 1, the speed can be calculated by the equation 6m ÷ 30s, which is 0.2m/s. For Car 2, the speed can be calculated by the equation 10m ÷ 30s, which is 0.33m/s. Therefore, the difference in average speed is 0.13m/s.

3.3 General advice for Section 3

3.3.1 How to prepare

Preparing for the Quantitative Reasoning section is extremely important due to the time constraints and variety of questions. To make the most of your preparation, you should do as many practice questions as you can online to become used to reading and answering questions on the computer while doing your working out on paper. As with Decision Making, this will also help you become faster with the on-screen calculator as it does have limitations and is somewhat clunky to use. As with most sections, you should begin by working through specific types of questions and becoming familiar with all the nuances and strategies you can use. It is important, however, to quickly build up to doing timed practice runs of this section before moving onto complete practice exams. Much like Verbal Reasoning, the time pressure is arguably the most difficult aspect, so it is much more valuable to do timed questions.

Something you should be aware of as you begin your preparation is that not all questions within Quantitative Reasoning neatly fall into a category of question you have seen before. As you will already know, questions involving percentages can be their own question type, yet often be assessing other skills such as interest calculations or physics conversions. While Quantitative Reasoning is often thought of as a fairly rigid and defined section, **adaptability** is very important as there is a broad number of topics encompassed by this section. You should always remember that it is the **problem solving skills,** not the actual maths itself, that is important. If you come across an unfamiliar question, it is tempting to flag it and move on as a method of saving time, but even spending a few seconds having a quick glance at the question stem could show you a way to find the solution. Obviously in the scenario that you are still unsure of how to proceed, it is best to be ruthless and continue making your way through the section without losing any momentum.

Completing Quantitative Reasoning practice questions will also allow you to hone your skills in **mental maths.** Using the calculator for quick and simple number crunching is not ideal due to the time-consuming nature of inputting numbers. Using your brain to do these tasks may be frustrating and inefficient at first, but with enough practice, you will find yourself saving a substantial amount of time. You will find that the best strategies to tackle each question type within the time limit often involve mental arithmetic along with efficient use of the on-screen calculator when necessary.

There are many times in the Quantitative Reasoning section where you will be forced to use the on-screen calculator. One of your goals in preparing for Quantitative Reasoning should be to make your calculator use as efficient as possible. Even saving a second per time your use the calculator will be extremely valuable and could give you enough time to answer at least another question over the course of completing the section. One of the best ways to use the on-screen calculator efficiently is to avoid using the mouse for inputting numbers. The mouse will always take longer than using the number keys on your keyboard, even if your typing speed isn't the best, so make sure to remember this for all your practice and it will become muscle memory by the time you have to sit the test. This will also be beneficial for your Decision Making preparation as many of the more numerical questions require calculator use.

By the end of your preparation, you should have a clear and rehearsed plan for each type of question that you can execute without error. Developing this requires careful analysis of your practice questions, including the questions you got right. It is particularly important that you change your approach if you find recurring errors, and keep searching for ways to streamline your method. Given the repetitive nature of Quantitative Reasoning questions, keeping a logbook of your mistakes could be a worthwhile investment of your time. Many of the questions you will find are basic and only require one or two steps, so thoughtless errors will be costly and frustrating, so you should be as thorough as possible, particularly if this aspect of mathematics has troubled you in the past.

3.3.2 Tips for staying on time

Staying on time is essential to maximise your results in the Quantitative Reasoning section of the UCAT. One of the ways you can increase your pace is by using **estimation.** The very nature of estimation means it is imprecise, and thus must be utilised cautiously as many questions do in fact require a fairly accurate answer.

There are two hints you can pick up on to decide whether to use an estimate to answer a question. Firstly, the question may simply tell you to make an estimate or approximation, although this is not particularly common. It is more likely you will have to check the answer options and decide if they are spaced out enough to exploit with estimation! The reason you want to use estimation is that round numbers make it quite easy to do mental maths, and in some cases allow you to answer the question by inspection. It takes a bit of practice to hone your judgement enough to consistently choose the optimal questions for exploitation, but it is well worth it.

Estimation is also useful when you have to analyse graphs as part of a question. Painstakingly figuring out where graphs line up on the axis is very time-consuming and often useless. If you see a graph, always look at the answer options and key words in the question stem as you should always be prioritising the estimation strategy unless there are explicit indicators to be precise. If you don't see any red flags, proceed with the question and estimate the values of the data points on the graph with a quick look at the axes, trying to make the numbers as conducive to mental maths as possible.

3.3.3 Running out of time

Quantitative Reasoning is a section where many people find themselves running out of time, but the numerical aspect makes it difficult to find shortcuts or use the technique of educated guessing. As discussed in the previous section, estimation is your best tool for staying on time, however the number-crunching still takes a while, and you may be in a position where you can only spend at most 10 to 15 seconds per question towards the end. Obviously, this is not ideal, but you can still make the best of it.

The main strategy at this point is to simply increase the chance that your random guess will be correct by eliminating as many answers as possible. As Quantitative Reasoning questions have five answer options, investing time in reducing this number will greatly improve your random guess accuracy.

One way to analyse answer options is to **look for a pattern.** If you find a few options that are linked by an operation such as a power of 10 in types of questions involving unit conversions or ratios, then you can immediately discount all other options as it is likely they are trying to trick students who haven't quite memorised the unit conversion numbers.

The same logic can be applied if you find a few answer options that are very close together in percentage questions, as the UCAT is trying to assess **numerical precision.** These strategies are clearly not always going to work, but if you have very limited time it is better to at least make an attempt to statistically boost your chances rather than become flustered and end up doing completely random guesses.

3.4 Strategy for associated questions

As with Verbal Reasoning and Decision Making, there are two question formats you can find in Quantitative Reasoning. It is important to note that these are substantially less distinct, as the question and answer arrangements are identical. The only difference is that some questions are linked by using the **same data or information,** while others are simply **standalone.** This may not seem like a worthwhile difference to observe, but you should adjust your strategy for each format to maximise your results. For now, we're going to dive into the first question format: associated questions.

It is important to note that associated question sets may not always utilise the *exact* same information. Occasionally, new information will be added for questions further into the set, or the information could be separate with the questions simply sharing a common theme. While this is not very common, you must be aware of this and treat them more like standalone questions if the information in the question stem is very different for each question. For the purposes of this section of the guide, we will only be discussing associated question sets that explicitly use identical data for every question in the set of four.

As with many question formats throughout the UCAT, associated questions should be considered **high-value** and form the bulk of the questions in Quantitative Reasoning since the information in the question stem is applicable to four questions. It's a simple matter of efficiency. You are better off analysing one section of data to answer four questions than one section of data to answer only one question.

When you start a new question with different information, you should always check forward to see if it is an associated chain of questions. Having a quick glance at the various questions will give you a good indication of where you should focus your attention when digesting the data before you get cracking with the first question.

If you find yourself getting bogged down, don't worry too much as you can afford to spend a bit more time when you are starting a chain of questions due to the unfamiliarity of the information. The subsequent questions also generally require the same skill or an extension of a skill, so spending extra time to lay the groundwork is not a waste.

The following set of associated questions is based on a tax table in the question, and demonstrate how different skills involving tax can be assessed through multiple questions requiring interpretation of the same data. This example also shows how repeated practice of important skills can allow you to quickly work through the more basic starting questions, giving you more time to tackle the later more advanced questions.

3.4 Strategy for associated questions

> **SAMPLE :**
> This table shows the total tax paid on annual taxable income.
>
> | Annual taxable income bracket (£) | Tax rate | Total tax paid at the top of this taxable income bracket (£) |
> |---|---|---|
> | 0 – 7,550 | 10% | 755 |
> | 7,550 – 23,250 | 15% | 3,110 |
> | 23,250 – 70,600 | 20% | 12,580 |
> | 70,600 – 155,150 | 30% | 37,945 |
> | 155,150 and over | 45% | |

Question 1: Ronald has an annual taxable income of £34,788. Correct to the nearest pound, how much income tax does he have to pay?

The first step is to work out which tax bracket this income fits into. Looking at the table, we can see it is in the third bracket, so we just need to add £3,110 onto the tax he accrues from his income above £23,250. If we subtract £23,250 from £34,788, it gives the result £11,538. As the tax rate in the third bracket is 20%, the tax on this income is £2,307.60. Adding this to £3,110 gives us the correct answer of £5,418 tax needing to be paid to the nearest pound.

Question 2: Claire has an annual taxable income of £77,890. Correct to the nearest pound, how much income tax does she have to pay?

This is basically the same question with different numbers. This often happens in Quantitative Reasoning, highlighting the importance of repetition and practice so you can have a robust and quick method to solve the basic questions. This income is in the fourth tax bracket, so we need to add £12,580 onto the tax she accumulates for income exceeding £70,600. Her income exceeding is £7,190 and is taxed at a rate of 30%, so her total tax can be calculated by adding £12,580 and £7,190 $\times 0.3$, giving us £14,737.

Question 3: Umesh has an annual taxable income of £208,345. Correct to three decimal places, what percentage of his income does he pay in tax?

It is around this point where the questions will start to extend the basic principles and ask you to complete more demanding tasks. In this case, the question is a simple extension of what we have been doing involving percentages. Using the same method as the previous two questions, we can calculate the tax he pays to be £61,882.75. Now we just need to work out what percentage of his taxable income this is by dividing £61,882.75 by £208,345 and multiplying by 100. Completing this gives the answer 29.702% correct to three decimal places. If you come across questions like this which require extreme precision, it is very important to always record your working out steps to more decimal places than the answer requires, as rounding during the working out stage can cause your answer to be slightly incorrect.

Question 4: Stuart pays £20,072 in tax per year. Correct to the nearest pound, what is his annual taxable income?

This is one of the more complex tax questions you can find, and unsurprisingly it is found at the end of a question set. Obviously, it is ideal to complete every question, but if you are struggling to find a way to break open a difficult question at the end of a set, then it could be worth moving on to give you more time to complete the easier questions at the beginning of a new associated question set. In order to start this question, you have to find out which tax bracket Stuart is in and then work backwards from there. Looking at the third column in the table, we know he must be in the fourth tax bracket and earn at least £70,600, accumulating £12,580 tax from this. Therefore he must be taxed £7,492 from the income he earns over £70,600. We know from the tax rate that this is 30% of his income above £70,600, so therefore he must earn £24,973.33 on top of this. Thus, his annual taxable income is £95,573.

3.5 Strategy for standalone questions

This next example demonstrates how to use data from a table in a set of questions that involve percentages. Working with percentages is incredibly important for many question types, and it can even be assessed in its own right, so familiarity is essential. While the content of this set of associated questions may not be difficult, using your calculator efficiently enough to complete the questions in the recommended time and being careful to avoid errors in data interpretation can be challenging.

SAMPLE:
The following table outlines the budget of a local government.

Allocation	Budget for 2026 (£m)	Increase over 2025 (£m)
Adult's social services	79	11
Children's social services	56	13
Infrastructure planning	43	4
Mental health investment	29	21
Waste management	27	2
Maintenance	13	0
Reserves	8	1
Total	255	

Question 1: What was the total budget for 2025?
This is a basic arithmetic question that should not trouble you. The method is simply to add all the increases over 2025 together and then subtract the total from the 2026 budget to give us £203 million.

Question 2: What was the percentage of the 2026 budget spent on mental health investment to the nearest percent?
Percentage calculations are the main focus of these kinds of question sets, so now we can start with the basic skill of conversion. We know that the spending on mental health investment in 2026 was £29 million, so we can divide that by the total budget of £255 million and multiply by 100 to get the answer 11% to the nearest percent.

Question 3: What percentage of the 2025 budget was allocated to Adult and Children's social services to the nearest percent?
We already know that the 2025 budget was £203 million from the first question and we can work out that in 2025, £111 million was allocated to Adult and Children's social services by adding the reduced amounts together. Therefore the percentage allocated to these services in 2025 was 55%.

Question 4: What is the percentage increase in spending from 2025 to 2026 correct to three decimal places?
In this question we have to use the information from the first question and also deal with percentages that are greater than 100. If we divide the 2026 budget by the 2025 budget and multiply by 100, then we can directly compare the budgets from a percentage perspective. Completing the calculation yields the result 125.616%. Now we know that the 2026 budget is 125.616% of the 2025 budget, we can figure out that there must have been a 25.616% increase in spending from 2025 to 2026.

3.5 Strategy for standalone questions

The second question format in the Quantitative Reasoning section of the UCAT is standalone questions, where the information contained within the stem is only relevant for one question, reducing its value significantly. Along with outlining the optimal strategy for approaching these questions, this section will also go through a couple of examples to enhance your understanding of Quantitative Reasoning questions and this particular presentation.

3.5.1 Saving time

As you will only be using the information in standalone questions to answer one question, an argument can be made that you should potentially flag and skip these questions to make the most of your time by doing associated question sets first and coming back at the end. Certainly, if you find yourself running out of time when you are doing timed practice runs of the Quantitative Reasoning section, this could be beneficial as it would allow you to complete as many questions as possible. This is not always the best approach, however, as often the standalone questions can be simpler or have less data in the question stem, making them easy marks. Nevertheless, it can be somewhat risky diving into a standalone question not knowing how long it will take you to complete.

A handy skill you should consider learning is being able to **quickly identify complex questions.** All the questions in Quantitative Reasoning are worth the same amount of marks, yet some questions require multiple steps of calculation, while others only need a simple check of a table of graph. This fundamental inequality can be exploited by prioritising fewer complex questions. This is similar to the strategy of prioritising associated question sets over standalone questions, but it adds another layer whereby you can categorise based on question difficulty and not just the amount of data needed for each question. Obviously, you will reach a point where analysing questions stops being beneficial, so in the end, it really depends on what you are comfortable with and works best for you. Ultimately, using the time-saving strategies mentioned earlier in this section of the guide along with lots of practice should ideally put you in a position where you can comfortably finish the Quantitative Reasoning section of the UCAT.

The follow example shows how to find the weighted mean in a question with data in the form of a table and the weightings not indicated explicitly. As we have already mentioned, you must be very confident in data interpretation so you can quickly adapt to the conditions of the question and apply the most efficient method.

SAMPLE:

This table outlines the cost of hiring a selection of builders and the amount of hours it will take each one to complete the task.

	Rate	Time to complete
Builder 1	£35/hour	12 hours
Builder 2	£25/hour	15 hours
Builder 3	£45/hour	8 hours

Question: What is the average hourly rate of the builders?

You can immediately tell from the question that it is asking for a mean, yet it may not be apparent that you have to calculate a *weighted* mean. The key is to recognise that the builders take a different amount of time so their respective costs cannot be weighted equally in the calculation for the average. The equation you must use to make the calculation can be derived from the data, and involves multiplying the rate for each builder by their time to complete the task and then dividing by the total time for all the builders. By doing the multiplication and adding the total costs for the builders, we obtain the number £1,155. To find the average hourly rate we just need to divide this by the total number of hours, which is 35. Doing this calculation yields the correct result £33/hour as the average rate.

As you can see, while this question is a standalone one and the information isn't as detailed compared to associated question sets, it doesn't take very long to complete with the right method. The trick is to quickly identify what kind of question it is, which is one of the most valuable passive benefits of practising a wide variety of Quantitative Reasoning under exam conditions.

3.5 Strategy for standalone questions

The final worked example in this section of the guide assesses your use of ratios and conversions. Ratios and unit conversions are common as standalone questions and can be time-consuming if you don't have an optimised method you have practised extensively. It is also imperative that you have memorised the diagram that shows you which power of 10 you need to use to convert distances, as confusion can arise in the heat of the moment. Here, the answer options are quite spaced out, giving you an opportunity to save a great deal of time by using estimation. But for the sake of completeness, we will demonstrate how to use both methods to complete this question.

> **SAMPLE:**
>
> A map of a farm shows a rectangular grazing paddock that measures 4 cm x 5.5 cm.
>
> The scale of the map is 1:40,000.
>
> 1 hectare = 10,000 m^2
>
> **Question: What is the area of the paddock in hectares?**
>
> (a) 3 hectares
> (b) 156 hectares
> (c) 352 hectares
> (d) 750 hectares
> (e) 3,520 hectares
>
> If we are to complete this question with the precise method, the first step is to convert each dimension of the grazing paddock into metres so you can calculate the area in metres^2. Using the scale, we know that the real-life dimensions of the paddock are 160,000 cm × 220,000 cm and these values can be converted into metres by dividing by 100. This gives us the dimensions 1,600 m × 2,200 m and an area of 3,520,000 m^2. Since 1 hectare is 10,000 m^2, we must divide the area of the paddock by 10,000 to convert it into hectares, giving us the answer of 352 hectares.
>
> Alternatively, the answers are spaced out enough to open up the possibility of using estimation to more efficiently obtain the correct answer. We can easily enough estimate that the real-life dimensions of the paddock are 150,000 cm × 200,000 cm through multiplication and then rounding out the numbers to make them easier to use. Converting this to metres gives us the dimensions 1,500 m × 2,000 m and the area calculation can be done in your head by multiplying 1.5 × 2 and then adding the required zeros to the result, giving 3,000,000 m^2. Removing the zeros in order to convert the answer to hectares leaves us with 300 hectares, and a clear answer of option C as we know we underestimated the result because we reduced both initial dimensions to make the calculations cleaner to complete mentally.
>
> Obviously this requires proficiency in mentally dealing with large numbers that have a lot of zeros, which can cause confusion in scenarios needing multiplication and division. However, it is definitely worth practising this estimation method as it can save valuable time in these situations. It is also possible to make an educated guess based on the answer options if you are really running out of time. You can pretty much disqualify Option A and Option E as they are orders of magnitude lower and higher than the rest of the options respectively, making it unlikely they are correct. From there, Option C seems the most likely correct answer as it a power of 10 away from Option E, opening up the possibility that they are testing how good your conversion skills are. Of course, this method is risky and certainly not foolproof, but it demonstrates that you can increase your chances of guessing correctly through a few seconds of basic analysis.

As you should be able to see by now, Quantitative Reasoning questions are heavily reliant on mathematical skills, yet at their core they are simply problem solving questions encoded in this often intimidating language. We would highly encourage you to brush up on your high school maths, but don't lose sight of what the UCAT really wants to assess with these questions. Now that we have covered all the content and question formats you can find in the Quantitative Reasoning section of the UCAT, we will leave you with two sample questions to further assist with your preparation and understanding of this section. Good luck!

3.6 Sample questions

SAMPLE:
The owner of a shopping centre wishes to collect data to improve customer service. The following table contains data from about how many hours customers spent in the shopping centre on a certain day.

Number of hours spent in shopping centre	Frequency
1	50
2	100
3	60
4	40

1. **What is the mean number of hours customers spend in the shopping centre?**
   - (a) 1.56
   - (b) 1.98
   - (c) 2.36
   - (d) 2.45
   - (e) 3.03

The owner also wishes to predict the customer growth that will occur in the following year. In 2018, the mean number of customers entering the shopping centre per day was 8,700. In 2019 it was expected that this mean would increase by 13%.

2. **What is the expected mean number of customers entering the shopping centre per day in 2019?**
   - (a) 7,600
   - (b) 9,831
   - (c) 9,994
   - (d) 10,000
   - (e) 10,338

There is a total of 84 stores in the shopping centre. Each store falls under one category according to the ratio 3:5:2:4, which corresponds to electronics, food, clothing, and hardware respectively.

3. **How many hardware stores are there in the shopping centre?**
   - (a) 24
   - (b) 26
   - (c) 28
   - (d) 30
   - (e) 32

The owner of the shopping centre decides to save £440,000 in an account which compounds 8% per annum.

4. **How much money will they have saved after four years?**
   - (a) £595,894.32
   - (b) £597,112.55
   - (c) £597,441.98
   - (d) £598,615.14
   - (e) £599,451.66

3.7 Answers to sample questions

> **SAMPLE :**
> Jeremy drives a powerful supercar. On one weekend, Jeremy drove his car from his home in the city to a distant town in the countryside. He left home at 8.00 a.m. and drove for 5 km on roads with a speed limit of 50 km/h. After that, he drove on roads with a speed limit of 80 km/h for 36 km. He then spent 2 hours at the town before driving back. Assume he maintained a steady maximum legal pace and drove back the same way he came.
>
> 5. What time did Jeremy arrive back at home?
>   - (a) 10.00 a.m.
>   - (b) 10.36 a.m.
>   - (c) 10.55 a.m.
>   - (d) 11.06 a.m.
>   - (e) 11.12 a.m.

3.7 Answers to sample questions

Question 1: C

As the question is asking for the mean and there are different frequencies attached to each hour, we can use the weighted mean formula. The equation $(50 \times 1 + 100 \times 2 + 60 \times 3 + 40 \times 4) \div 250$ can be derived from the data in the table. This gives us the answer 2.36.

Question 2: B

As this is a percentage question, we can simply use the equation $8,700 \times 1.13$ to find that the answer is 9,831.

Question 3: A

Adding together the parts of the ratio gives a sum of 14. Dividing the total number of stores, 84, by 14 gives us the factor 6. Now we have a link between the ratio and absolute number of stores, we can multiply the part of the ratio corresponding to hardware stores by this factor. According to the ratio, 4 of the 14 parts are for hardware stores, so therefore the number of hardware stores in the shopping centre is 24.

Question 4: D

You can either plug the numbers into the compound interest formula or work through each year until you reach the answer. Using the latter method, you can simply multiply the initial investment of £440,000 by 1.08 and then multiply the result by 1.08, repeating the initial step another two times to simulate four years of compounding interest. This gives the precise answer of £598,615.14 and is arguably less tedious than employing the compound interest formula.

Question 5: D

If Jeremy drives for 5 km at 50km/h, then we can find the time it took by dividing distance by speed and multiplying by 60 to find the time in minutes. This gives us a running total of 6 minutes for this leg of the journey. Applying the same method for the next part of the journey, where Jeremy drives for 36 km at 80 km/h gives us 27 minutes as the time taken. Therefore, the total time taken for the journey to the town is 33 minutes. As he spends 2 hours at the town and uses the exact same route back to his house, the time taken for the entire journey is 3 hours and 6 minutes. As he leaves at 8.00 a.m., this means he must have arrived back at his house at 11.06 a.m.

Section 4

Section 4 – Abstract Reasoning

4.1 Introduction

Following Quantitative Reasoning, the fourth section of the UCAT is called Abstract Reasoning. It starts with 1 minute for reading the instructions and only 13 minutes of test-taking time to answer all 55 questions. Given that you only have around 14 seconds on average for each question, this section arguably imposes the greatest amount of time pressure. This is an assessment of your capacity to expertly **recognise patterns within a group of abstract shapes** and accompanying distractions that, if proper deduction skills are not applied, may mislead you from the correct conclusion. Abstract Reasoning also looks at whether you can back-track or change track in pattern identification, and whether you can create and critically appraise hypotheses.

Despite the fact that questions requiring you to deal with a string of random shapes seem irrelevant to the scientific field of Medicine, this judgement overlooks the deeper qualities that this section evaluates. In their everyday life, doctors constantly employ their ability of **pattern recognition and identification of distracting factors.** They are given a list of symptoms and test results from a patient to help them with considering differential diagnoses. Some of the given information may form a pattern that indicates a certain medical condition and is most likely what the patient presents with, whilst the rest may remain unclear or even stray towards a completely irrelevant conclusion that, if considered, will not help the patient or may even worsen their condition.

For example, consider a patient presenting with chest pain, dizziness, and breathing difficulties. All three of these symptoms can point to a heart attack, but they can also be symptoms of a panic attack, which would indicate a mental health issue rather than a cardiac issue, hence requires a completely different approach to treatment and management. A good doctor will recognise this pattern and the multiple conclusions it leads to, and will consequently probe the patient with more questions in order to shorten the list of differential diagnoses until a final diagnosis and treatment plan can be made. Medical practitioners need to make judgements about the wide range of information given to them, whether it be from the patient themselves or from laboratory tests, and identify and sort the information which will assist their deductions. In addition, medical research involving producing and handling data requires one to gauge patterns so that we can produce more hypotheses to test in the future.

In the Abstract Reasoning section of the UCAT, there will be **four question types** present amongst the 55 questions in total.

1. For the first type, you are given two groups of shapes called '**Set A' and 'Set B',** then you are provided with a '**Test Shape**' and asked whether it belongs to *Set A, Set B,* or *Neither.*
2. The second type are the '**Next in the Sequence**' questions where you are given a sequence of shapes and asked to pick which shape amongst your options should be next in the series.
3. In the third question type, you are provided with a statement **(Shape A is to Shape B, as Shape C is to ?)** that includes a group of shapes and subsequently a list of possible shapes to complete the statement.
4. The fourth type is similar to the first – you are given two groups of shapes called '**Set A' and 'Set B'**, except now you are given four options and asked to pick **which option belongs to Set A or B.**

These questions types will be intermingled throughout the section and will not strictly appear in this order, nor is there necessarily the same amount of questions distributed evenly for each question type. As such, it's important to be equally comfortable with each question type to ensure you can approach this section with confidence.

4.2 Core skills

4.2.1 Pattern recognition

Pattern recognition happens when you receive information (in this case, visual information is received by your eyes) and your brain stores it temporarily in your short-term memory, at which point your long-term memory is subsequently activated. In doing so, your mental perception of the received information is enhanced by remembering and being able to apply what is familiar or what was the experience in a previous similar circumstance. For example, if you complete a practice *Set A, B, or Neither* question which involved arrows, and the pattern for that question was that an arrow always pointed to a square, the next time you encounter a Section 4 question containing arrows, you would be more inclined to check whether it points to something specific. Having this skill is quite self-explanatory, but it will greatly aid you in terms of the speed and efficiency with which you can detect patterns, in what can otherwise be perceived as a mess of abstract objects. Being able to **draw connections between different elements, based on a variety of features,** is the fundamental ability being tested in this section, but the **highly restrictive time limit** adds a challenge of how rapidly you can use this ability. To build this skill, the most helpful method is to just keep practising with different combinations of components, shapes, and relationships. With enough practice, you will start to notice common patterns appearing again and again, and your radar for identifying possible connections will greatly improve. In fact, it will become much easier to figure out patterns that you may have never encountered before, due to your increased familiarity with the vastly different ways shapes can appear and the way shapes can move to create a pattern.

4.2.2 Time management

The Abstract Reasoning section of the UCAT is arguably the trickiest section in relation to timing, with only 13 minutes for 55 questions. The time goes by in a flash, so being able to allocate your time wisely to each question will assist your performance in such time-restricted conditions. Depending on your strengths, you should alter the amount of time you give each question type, such as allocating slightly more time for 'Set A/B/Neither' questions and much less time for 'Next in the Sequence' questions. Usually, a good time limit to give yourself is a **maximum of one minute before moving on to the next question.** This is because if you end up spending 4 minutes on a particularly difficult question, you will have lost about one-third of the total time you have for the entire section!

4.3 General advice for Section 4

The most important piece of advice that is applicable for all question types in this section is to **avoid rushing to get the answer** and instead take your time! Of course, there is a rigid and demanding time limit, but it must be considered that one pattern, such as the pattern for Set A and Set B for the first question type, can be used for multiple questions, usually four or five. Once you understand a pattern, having spent a little extra time dedicated towards the methodical thinking, you can easily and efficiently go through all the questions associated with the pattern at a much faster rate. This is especially true in comparison to someone skimming over the pattern superficially, looking at the questions and trying to come up with possible associations and patterns via trial and error for each question. The latter is more likely to lead to extra time being wasted between each question, and hence greater anxiety with being able to finish the rest of the questions in time. This panicked state of mind, if not battled with exam relaxation techniques, can cause foggier thinking that will likely obscure other patterns and lead to more frustration, and this cycle will just keep going until time runs out! To avoid this, ensure you **focus on understanding a pattern first,** and if you can't work it out after a minute, move on to the next question.

Next, you should **note down the patterns** you observe in the question stem, particularly if it is a 'Set A and Set B' question type. Since you will be provided with a booklet and pen for working out, use these to their full extent to jot down any detected patterns and similarities. For instance, in a 'Set A, B or Neither' question, if you observe that all of the boxes in Set A have two black squares, immediately write this down and compare with Set B, which may only have one black square for each box. This gives you a physical reference point to look at to compare the 'Test Shape' or the options provided, making it much easier to detect which options must be eliminated and which is the correct answer.

To be efficient in the way you do this and make the most of your test-taking time, write down the patterns using a **shorthand system** that you understand. For example, if one pattern you observed involves the fact that all the squares in Set A have 3 white circles while Set B's squares all have 5 white circles, you can write this down as: "A = 3 W ◯, B = 5 W ◯." Create this shorthand system as you go through practice questions and implement them during your practice exams, under timed exam conditions, to ensure that utilising this system in the real exam comes as naturally as possible.

With the sheer number and variety of abstract shapes and other elements which a question may contain, it may be confusing to know where to start looking for a pattern. This applies particularly to the first and fourth question type, involving a Set A and Set B, where you will be looking for the primary similarity that marks a test shape as belonging to either group can be bewildering. A good acronym that can help you break down the large and complex arrangements is **SCANS**, which stands for **Shape, Colour, Angle/Arrangement, Number** and **Size/Symmetry**. Here is a list of even more specific features to look for!

Shape	– Type (irregular or regular; square, rectangle, triangle, etc.) – Edges (straight, curvy) – Angles (acute, right, obtuse) – Open or Closed (whether the edges enclose the shape or not)
Colour	– Presence of shading (fully, partly or not shaded) – Level of shading (fully black, dark grey, grey, light grey, white) – Number of colours (four black, three white, etc.)
Angle/ arrangement	– Position (right, left, top, bottom, centre) – Rotation (45°, 90°, 135°, 180°) – Movement (clockwise, anti-clockwise; increments) – Arrows (pointing to something specific, angles) – A shape always being inside another shape – Arrangement relative to another shape (e.g. if a square has a big cross inside it, then the shapes at each of the four ends of the cross are rotated by 90 degrees, or there is always a square next to a triangle) – Mirroring (does a particular shape mirror itself or another across a horizontal, vertical, or diagonal line?) – Overlap/intersections (does a particular shape always intersect or overlap with another shape of the same or different kind?)
Number	– Total shapes in a square – Total of a specific type of shape – Sides – Angles – Gaps – Odd or even – Intersections – Areas/regions formed – Number of one shape relative to the number of another shape (number of white shapes = number of black shapes +3, number of triangles + number of squares = number of circles, etc.) – Ratios (e.g. the number of triangles to rectangles is in the ratio of 1:3)
Size/symmetry	– Small/medium/large – One particular component small or big in each box – One component the same or a different size every time it appears in a box – Line of symmetry across the square (horizontal, vertical, diagonal, none) – Entirely symmetrical or just one component – Each shape has one or two lines of symmetry

The above list of the specific features under each of the five categories of SCANS may seem overwhelming at first, but it should be wired into your head with enough practice. So do not worry about memorising this entire table before starting practice questions. By exposing yourself to as many questions and an **expansive variety of patterns,** all of these particular details will become like a routine, as a quick check-list to tick off as you go.

In your UCAT practice for this section, try and do as many questions as you can, from a variety of sources. This increases your sense of **familiarity with different question types** and gets you into the practice of finding patterns a lot quicker, and you may find that the same patterns keep turning up for different questions, and you will be able to build a **mental bank of all the different rules that a question may involve.**

For example, by doing many 'Next in the Sequence' questions, your eyes can detect the likely movements of different elements and associate them with all the different patterns you would have already been exposed to. For instance, suppose one of the first 'Next in the Sequence' questions you did at the very start of your UCAT preparation was the question below.

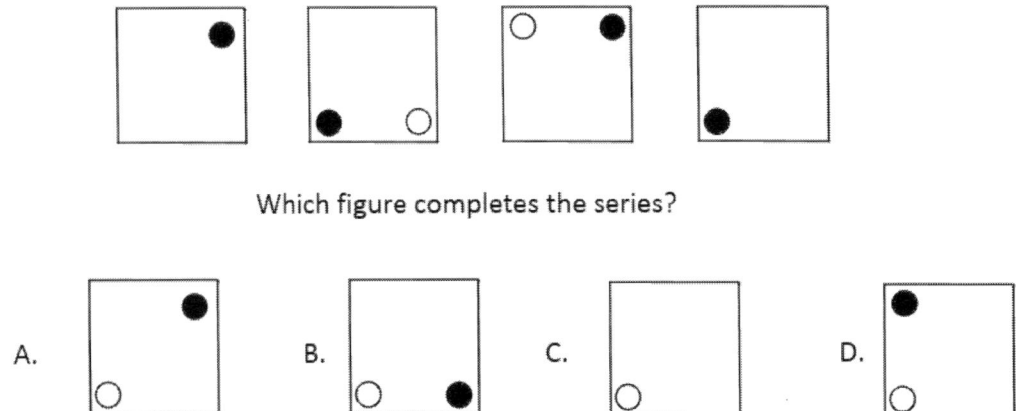

Which figure completes the series?

The first thing you may notice is the fact that the black circle always appears either in the top right corner or bottom left corner, which can lead you to eliminate options B and D. This makes the pattern for the black circle being that it alternates between each of these corners, so the next in the series must have a black circle in the top right corner (automatically leading you to the answer, which is option A). Assuming that black circles overlap white circles, you can then make the assumption that the white circle is travelling using the 1-2-3-4 pattern clockwise, where it moves one corner, then moves two corners, and so on. Ultimately, the fifth square should have a white circle in the bottom left corner, which confirms the answer to be option A. If you can use the process of elimination with the black circle alone, you do not need to go ahead and ensure that the white circle is meant to be in its correct position in your chosen answer as well – time is of the essence after all!

After doing lots of questions of this type, you will become automatically inclined to go through your mental bank of patterns, such as if a particular shape only touches opposite corners (as was the case above), and the thinking process that will lead you to your final answer will be much quicker. This enables you to be able to tackle questions of the same type but higher in difficulty, an example of which is shown on the following page.

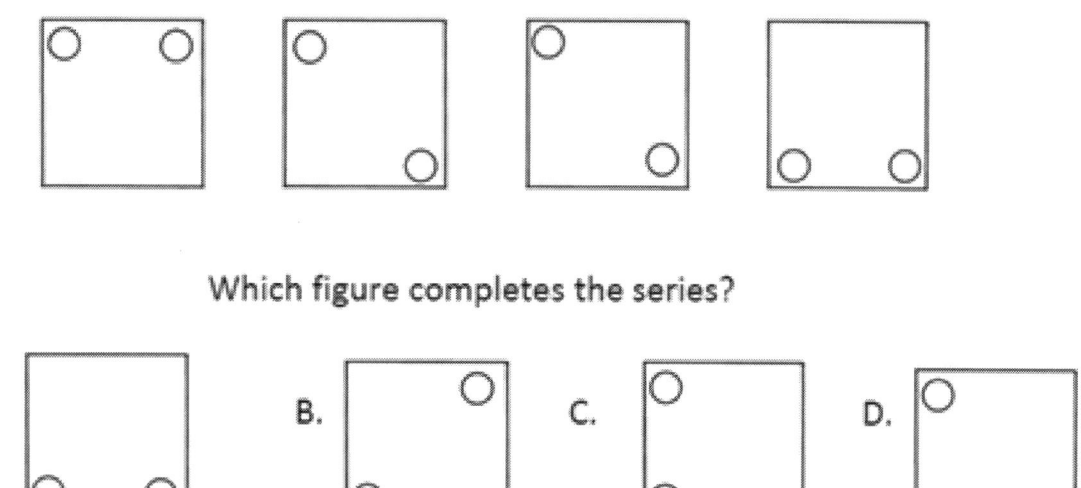

Which figure completes the series?

A.   B.   C.   D.

You may initially be thrown off by the presence of two white circles and find keeping track of them is harder than having two distinct elements (like the black and white circle in the previous example). However, from the copious practice questions you would have done by this point, you would try to look for a simple pattern. Something you might have noticed is that no circle touches the bottom left corner, but there is always a circle in either the top left corner or bottom right corner. So you can consider the circle in the top left corner for the first box to be alternating opposite corners, and (though this would be time consuming in the actual UCAT exam) you can visually differentiate this by copying the series onto the provided booklet and drawing a cross in this particular circle (as shown below). This then makes tracking the pattern for this individual circle and separating it from the other circle much easier.

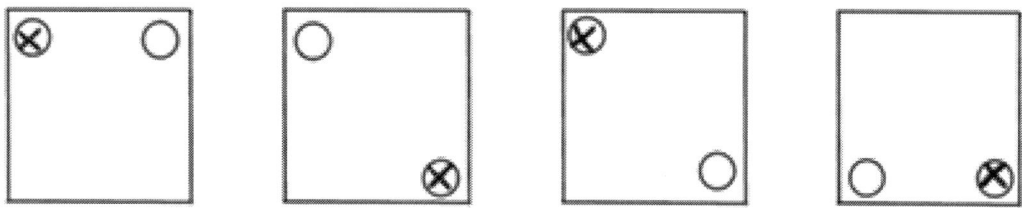

Now you should quickly recognise the positioning of the white circle to be that of the 1-2-3-4 pattern going anti-clockwise. This makes it so that the answer should have a circle (the circle with the cross in it) in the top left corner and the other white circle in the bottom left corner, which gives us option C.

However, there are many potential tricks and traps in the Abstract Reasoning section – the two main ones are **distractors** and **conditional patterns.** The first type, distractors, are elements which have intrinsically **no link** whatsoever to the pattern itself, and so try to mislead you from the path of getting to the correct answer. Since distractors are present in all four question types in Abstract Reasoning, these will start to pop up after doing a lot of general practice, where you will be able to quickly change your hypotheses to test another possible pattern. Conditional patterns are where the state or character of one component is **reliant on the traits of another component.** Although these factors are typically only present in the really difficult Abstract Reasoning questions and are not too common overall, it is important to look out for these once you cannot find a straightforward pattern. The ability to pick up on distractors and conditional patterns is even more valuable if you are aiming for a very high score in this section, as this will help you to stand out from the rest of the candidates.

As we'll later explore in the section on advice for sitting the UCAT on page 88, during the minute provided when you are meant to read the instructions, you should jot down important notes that will help you keep up with the speed required to potentially finish all the questions on time. More specifically, for this section, you should memorise or else write down the mnemonic **SCANS** or even make your own acronym based on all the patterns you have encountered, particularly ones which are the most common (such as the total number of shapes for Set A/B/Neither questions or the 1-2-3-4 rule for 'Next in the Sequence' questions).

4.3 General advice for Section 4

4.3.1 How to prepare

To start your preparation, you should begin with questions of simpler nature and lower difficulty, with patterns that are more apparent at a glance, then attempt those of gradually increasing complexity. For example, as a question that you may begin your preparation with, consider the shapes below.

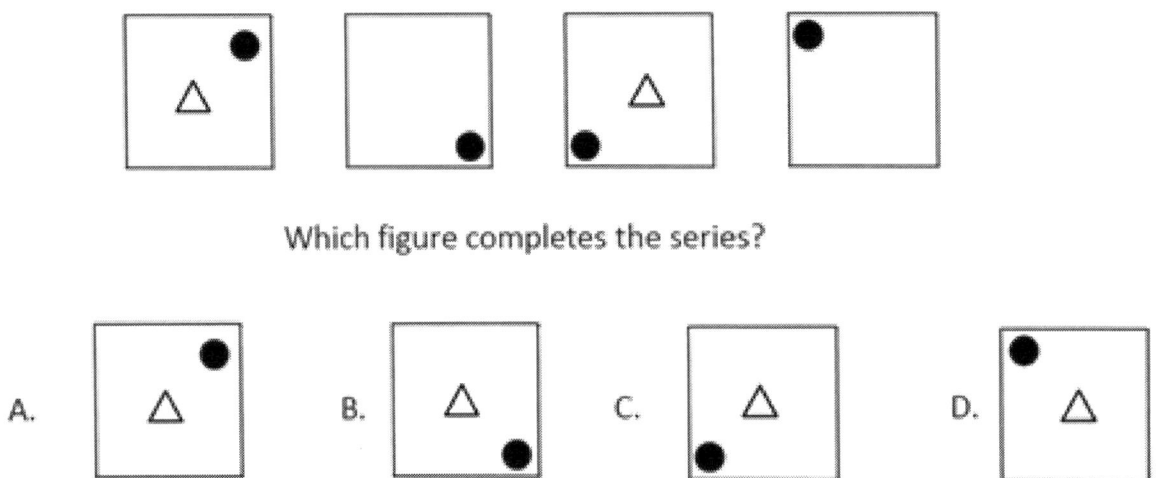

The elements present are a white triangle and a black circle. You will notice that the triangle appears in the first square and third square, but not the other two. So, you can assume from here that this component alternates every second square, thus leading to the prediction that it will appear in the fifth square. Looking at your options, they all have the centre white triangle present, therefore you cannot eliminate any alternatives with this information alone. Now, observing the black circle, you will see that it starts at the top right corner, then appears in the bottom right corner, then the bottom left corner and finally the top left corner. From here comes the rule that this component moves one corner clockwise, therefore the square that should come next needs this element to be in the top right corner, leading to the answer which is option A.

Since this particular series had only two patterns in total present amongst its components, it can be considered quite easy compared to what you can find in the real exam, where there may be multiple layers of arrangements and up to five or more patterns in total, many of which will be fairly subtle.

The Abstract Reasoning section of the UCAT is arguably the easiest section for students to improve in, so ensure you **understand the patterns and underlying concepts** behind each type of practice question before continuing on with the next. This means looking carefully at the worked solutions for every question you do and analysing the thought process of the person who had created the question. Perhaps their way of getting to the answer is starkly different from how you approached the question, either leading you to the wrong answer or to the correct answer but in a slower and less efficient way. The latter case will help you broaden your network of how to tackle different question types, making your approach much more effective as you would have found techniques that take less time to go through than your own initial reasoning.

More importantly, by reviewing your performance during your practice, you can analyse the kind of questions that you answer incorrectly most of time. Ask yourself **where you are going wrong** in these cases. Do you keep forgetting a specific component of SCANS? Do you keep getting duped by a particular exam trick? By going through this introspection, you can identify the pattern (pun unintended) that you keep falling into and address it accordingly, such as ensuring that it is the first thing you look for in a given question.

Collate a **list of patterns** as you go along with your practice, whether it be handwritten in a notebook or typed up in a Word Document or OneNote. Use this list for when you do your practice questions, so that you can gradually embed them into your mind and apply them with greater ease during practice exams and the real exam. The following is an example of an excerpt of a list that a candidate could have collected over their preparation period.

4.3.2 List of pattern types

Pattern	Question type	Example
Moving every 1/2/3 corners/steps	Next in the Sequence	
Moving 1 corner, then 2 corners (or 2 corners then 1 corner)	Next in the Sequence	
Alternating corners	Next in the Sequence	
One corner/place forward, two corners/places back	Next in the Sequence	
Moving 1 corner, then 2, then 3, then 4	Next in the Sequence	
Angles moving: 45, 90, 135, 180	Next in the Sequence	
Angles moving 45, 90, 180, 360	Next in the Sequence	
Total number	Set A, B or Neither/Pick Which Set	

4.3 General advice for Section 4

While we have already gone through the different question types in Abstract Reasoning, it is likely that such patterns will appear across multiple question types. The types listed in the table below are where each pattern appears most commonly. Realistically, drawing and including an example for each of these cases can be difficult and time-consuming, so instead you can simply write in words each of the patterns you come across. Below is an example.

Pattern	Question type (in which it appears)
Total number for a specific shape	*Set A, B or Neither/Pick Which Set*
All shapes have curved edges or straight edges (in a set)	*Set A, B or Neither/Pick Which Set*
Certain type of shape (e.g. circle) is in the top right or left	*Set A, B or Neither/Pick Which Set*
Number of intersections between two or more lines	*Set A, B or Neither/Pick Which Set*
Odd or even number of lines that come out of a certain shape	*Set A, B or Neither/Pick Which Set*
Grey shapes are one or two spaces away from white shapes	*Set A, B or Neither/Pick Which Set*
Shape/arrow flips in second image	*Complete the Statement*
Shape/arrow rotates 45° or 90° clockwise or anti-clockwise	*Complete the Statement*
Black turns to white, and vice versa, in second image	*Complete the Statement*
The second box has one more enclosed region in each of the shapes it contains than the first box (e.g. if the first box had a triangle with two lines through it, meaning it has three enclosed spaces, the second box may have any shape, such as another triangle or even a square, with three lines through it, meaning it now has four enclosed spaces)	*Complete the Statement*
One shape is inside a bigger shape, but positions swap in second image (for example, if a small triangle is inside a big square, in the second image a small square will be inside a big triangle)	*Complete the Statement*

Finally, try to do all of your preparation for this section **on a computer,** rather than on paper. Perhaps, if it helps you to get more comfortable with the format of this section, you can start your preparation on paper, but switch to computer or laptop as soon as possible. The reason for this is that this most closely resembles how the real exam will work, and you don't want to be thrown off by the computer-based nature when it counts. For instance, if you keep practising on paper, you have the ease of directly annotating the shapes with a pencil or pen in the question booklet. However, in the real exam, you may have to draw out the shapes on the booklet and then annotate them, whilst switching your attention between the paper and the computer screen, leading to precious seconds being wasted. Practising on a computer will also force you to be more conscious of the time, while practising on paper using books makes forgetting about the time a lot easier.

4.4 Strategy for type 1: *Set A, B, or Neither* questions

In this question type, you are given **two sets of six squares** and each set is either labelled Set A or Set B. The squares contain abstract shapes, which may seem randomly arranged at first but they all contain **at least one similar characteristics** that makes them belong to their designated set. It is your task to find the element(s) that determine whether a box belongs to Set A or B. Under a given pair of Set A and Set B, there are multiple questions (often three to six) where you are provided with a **Test Shape,** which is just another square containing abstract shapes, and asked to choose if it belongs to Set A, Set B, or neither. It is probably a bit hard to visualise the format of this type of question using just words as a description, so below is an example of what this may look like.

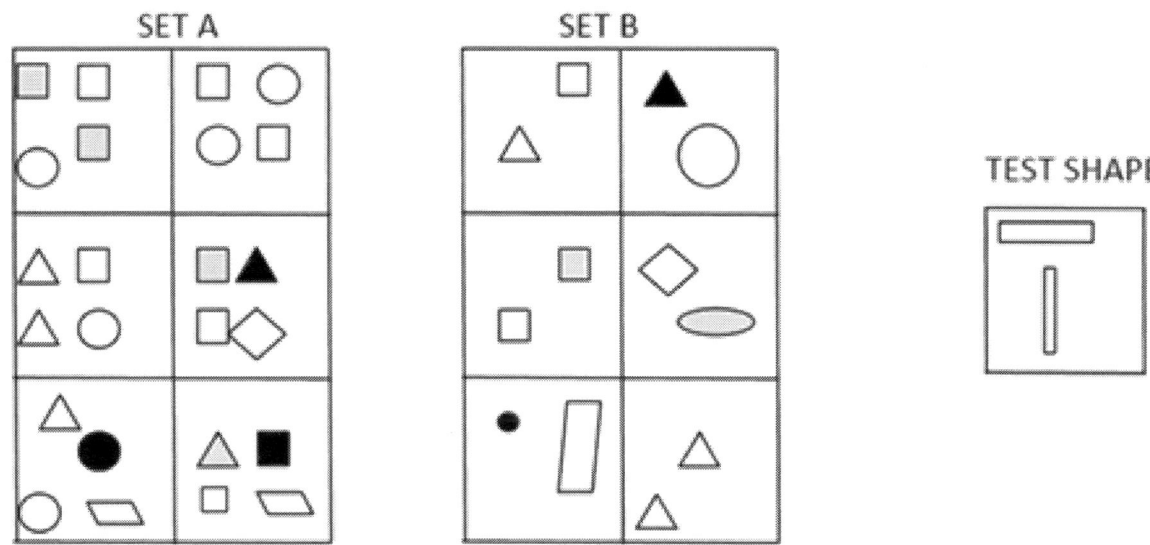

You will only be given three possible options to choose from for each of these questions: **Set A, Set B or Neither.** Since *Neither* is an option, the process of elimination becomes a bit harder. This reinforces the fact that you should become familiar with and master the process of **finding patterns quickly** in any given pair of sets.

It may be tempting to look for an order in which a possible pattern may flow. In other words, you may start with the top left square and try to look for a pattern that progresses horizontally or vertically across, especially if the boxes contain arrows and shapes turning in different angles. However, it must be understood that in this question type there is **no order within the sets** to be followed and the only thing that is holding each of the six squares together in a set is the range of particular characteristics that they share with other squares in the set, which separate them from the other set.

When determining what possible rules that a set might follow, try to **avoid patterns that involve 'at least,'** such as 'for a square to belong in Set A, it must have at least one triangle'. This rule is way too broad and is highly likely to be applicable to both sets, which will not help you differentiate which set a given Test Shape belongs to, (assuming it belongs to either). This also applies to **rules which are negative,** like 'all the squares in Set A do **not** contain a striped diamond', where the possibilities are endless. Instead, aim for **positive, specific rules** such as 'all the squares in Set A contain a striped diamond.'

Another important thing to keep in mind is that **the main pattern that is present in Set B is either the opposite or similar to that of Set A.** For example, Set A's rule may be that there is always one black triangle in each square and Set B's rule is that instead there is always one black rectangle. Another example could be that there is a big central arrow for each square in each set, and for Set A, the arrow always points to a corner, while for Set B, the arrow always faces the edge of the square instead.

4.4 Strategy for type 1: Set A, B, or Neither *questions*

A general rule is that **if a pattern works in three boxes, then it is likely applicable to the rest of the squares.** Remembering this will save you heaps of time as you won't have to confirm the rule for all six squares every time. However, to be safe, try to quickly check if the pattern you proposed works in four or five boxes in total. You should keep this in mind for all of your Set A/B/Neither questions, but fall back on checking just three boxes when you are very short of time.

Another useful piece of advice is to **start from the simplest square,** regardless of its position in its relative set (whether it be top left or middle right – since order does not matter!). From here, observe **what is different between your chosen box and the box that is slightly more complex.** To illustrate this point, refer to the sets and 'Test Shape' shown below.

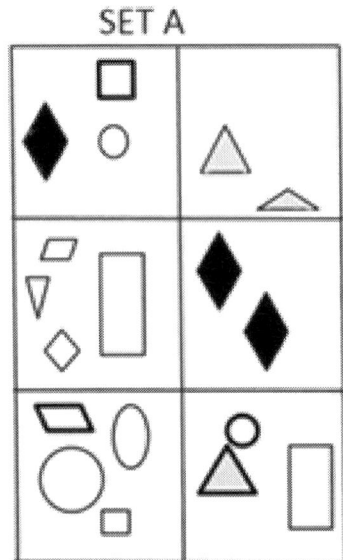
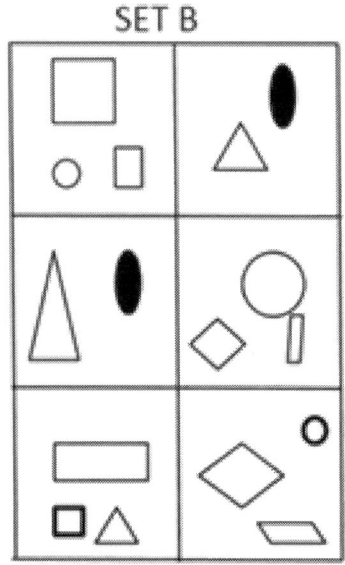
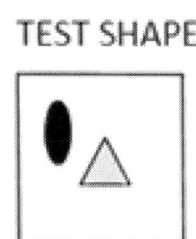

You are provided with an assortment of different shapes, including triangles, boxes, circles, ovals, rectangles, parallelograms, rhombuses, and diamonds. In addition, some of these shapes have been fully coloured or shaded grey and others have a thick outline. Seeing all of this at first glance may be befuddling and your mind may try to tackle the plausible relationships between the shading and outlining of a shape all at once, when this information may not be relevant in the first place. So, let us start with the simplest shape in Set A, which is the middle left square, and compare it with the second-most simple square, which is the bottom left square. The first thing you notice is the fact that both squares have four shapes, so from here, you can try the possible pattern that all Set A squares have four shapes. In this case, it can be assumed that there is no pattern relating to the thickness of a shape's outline, since both aforementioned squares contain four shapes regardless. Next, we can look at the bottom right square, and we notice that there are two white shapes and a grey triangle instead. Similarly, the top left square has two white shapes (one being a thickly outlined square, but remember that we ruled out outline thickness as a crucial factor) and a black diamond instead. Before eliminating the overriding rule we predicted, since both of these squares have only three shapes in total rather than four, we can consider whether being coloured or shaded has an important role. Since the other two squares (top right and middle right) have only two of each coloured shape, let us test whether a shape being coloured equates its value to two white shapes. If this is the case, then the top left square and bottom right square still have a value of four white shapes, and the same applies to the other two squares. Therefore, using a shorthand system, we can jot down something like:

Set A: 4 (B diamond/G triangle = 2)
i.e. Set A contains shapes that add up to a value of 4
(the black diamond and the grey triangle are equal to two shapes each)

4.5 Strategy for type 2: Next in the Sequence *questions*

You should then apply the same process of thinking for Set B, since the pattern in Set B is usually either the opposite of or similar to what happens in Set A. In doing so, you will then observe that a black oval equates to 2 white shapes, making the pattern that all Set B squares must contain a value of three white shapes. Writing this in shorthand may look like the following.

Set B: 3 (B oval = 2)

Now looking at the Test Shape, you will see that it contains both a black oval and a grey diamond. Considering that both of these shapes equates to two white shapes, the value of the box overall is three white shapes (since we cannot assume that a black oval equates to two white shapes in Set A, and vice versa for the grey diamond in Set B – they are each relevant only to their relative set). This then leads straight to the answer that the Test Shape belongs to Set B, according to our rule that all boxes in Set B must have the value of three white shapes.

To combine the above two points (looking at the simplest square first and checking if a pattern works in three squares), you can use something called the **Three Square Rule.** This is where you start with the simplest box, then look at the two boxes directly adjacent to it. All the squares in a set follow the exact same rule, so beginning with the simplest box will leave you with the fewest distractors that could otherwise throw you off from the start. Then, you should compare the three boxes in terms of similarities regarding their **shapes, colour, edges, positioning, angles, patterns,** and so on. While you should check the pattern you have come up with works in the other three boxes for the same set, what is more important is that you check if it **does not work for any of the boxes in the other set.**

Along with looking at the simplest square, you must focus on **one possible pattern at a time,** especially if there are multiple elements present within each set. This will help prevent you from getting overwhelmed with the complex shapes and interactions within each square, and instead promotes a logical approach to getting the final answer. In other words, multiple rules often exist, but you should not focus on finding every single one of these right away. Simply finding one or two rules should be sufficient with helping you sorting the Test Shape into its correct place.

If you get stuck with a question and experience difficulty with finding any trace of a pattern, you should try to look at the two sets from a **bird's eye perspective.** Zooming out and seeing both sets from a distance – as a larger picture rather than twelve individual squares – can help make a pattern become more obvious. For instance, you may have been focusing so much on the minor details of a set (like the angles which two arrows make), when the pattern was simply that there was always a square directly adjacent to two triangles.

4.5 Strategy for type 2: *Next in the Sequence* questions

For this question type, you are provided with four individual shapes (usually squares, but they can be other shapes, such as a series of four hexagons), each with a set of abstract elements, and these squares **follow an order depending on the pattern that governs them.** Under the question stem, you are provided with **four options,** each with a square that contains the same or similar elements to those found in the given series, and you are asked to choose which one completes the series.

The primary advice for this section is to **look at one piece or component present within the shapes at a time and track its movement through the sequence.** Whilst this has been said before, this tip has greater significance to this question type, particular since the order formed by the placement of these pieces matter. Use the table and diagrams of the list of possible patterns on page 57 to guide you with identifying how each individual component is linked to one another.

4.5 Strategy for type 2: Next in the Sequence *questions*

Below, we will go through a worked example, but you can try to answer it yourself first!

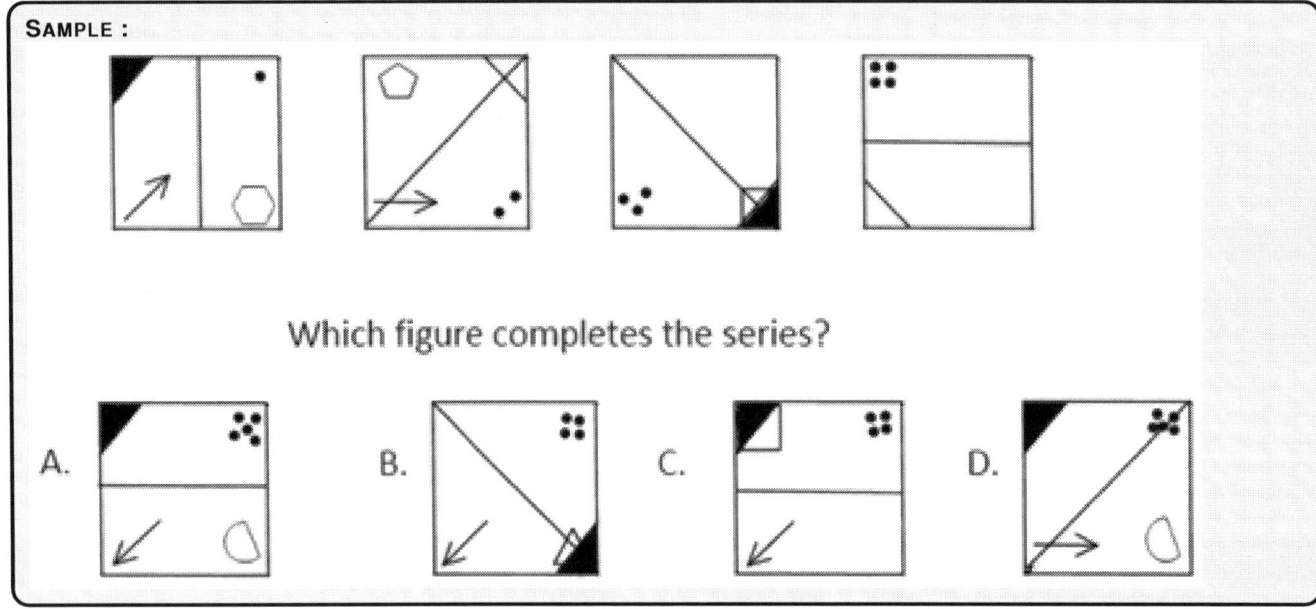

Here, there are five individual components at work. The first one we will look at is the big line that goes across the entire square. This line is rotating around the square clockwise using the 45-90-135-180 rule, where it first rotates 45 degrees, then rotates 90 degrees from the square that is directly previous to the current square, and so on. To help identify this rule, try marking the top of the line (in the first square) with a circle or a cross and follow its movement along the sequence. Below is a way in which you can do this, along with dotted lines of the previous position, annotations of the angles and a rough drawing of the position of the line in the fifth square (hence what to look for amongst the answer options).

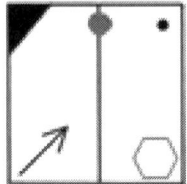 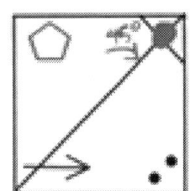 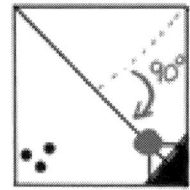 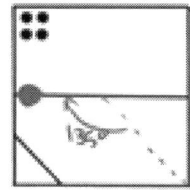 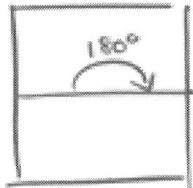

Since the line must go through the square horizontally, we can rule out options B and D. The next component that is visible in all four squares is the set of dots, which have two separate patterns. Firstly, the number of dots in this group increases by one, so the fifth square must have five dots, and secondly, this group moves one space clockwise, meaning that it should be present in the top right corner. You would have also noticed that the triangle in the corner not only alternates between being black and white but also moves one corner clockwise, meaning that it lands in the top left corner as black. Next, there is the arrow which stays in the bottom left corner and has evidently rotated by 45 degrees from the first square to the second. However, just from this, we cannot say for sure if it moves just by 45 degrees or if it follows the 45-90-135-180 rule. We can test these two hypotheses, where the arrow is diagonal and points to the bottom right (or south-east) if it uses the 45-90-135-180 rule, or points to the bottom left (or south-west) if it only rotates by 45 degrees. The latter is seen to be true since none of the options contains the position required for the 45-90-135-180 rule to be applied. Finally, the shape present in the square decreases in the number of edges by one and alternates between the bottom right and top left corner. Thus, our answer is option A.

4.6 Strategy for type 3: *Complete the Statement* questions

In this section, you are provided with three complete big squares and one blank big square, with the first two squares having the same relationship or pattern as the last two squares. For each pair of big squares, the second square is followed by the first square with the phrase "is to." Refer below for a basic illustration of what this looks like.

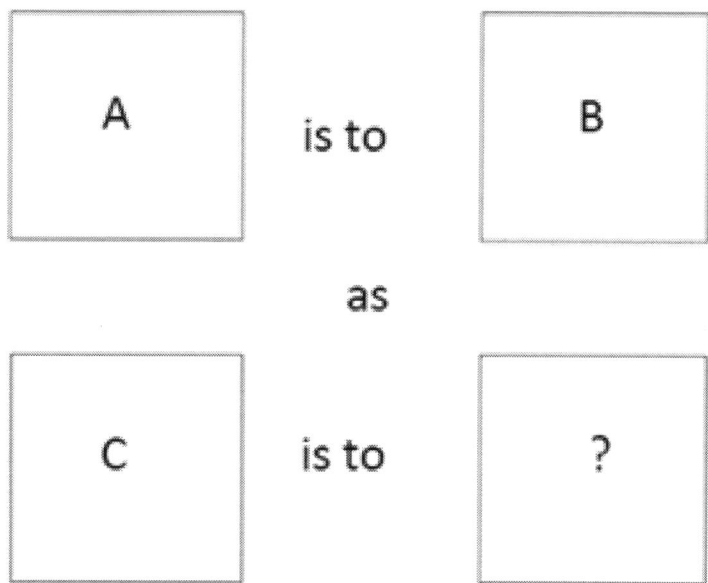

Your job is to figure out what leads to the square B being made from A (e.g. are all the shapes which were white in square A now turned black in square B?) and then apply these rules to square C to get square D from your list of four possible options (e.g. the two white squares and three white triangles in square C will now all be black in square D)

The following is a worked example of a this type of question; try and find the pattern yourself before looking at the worked solutions on the following page!

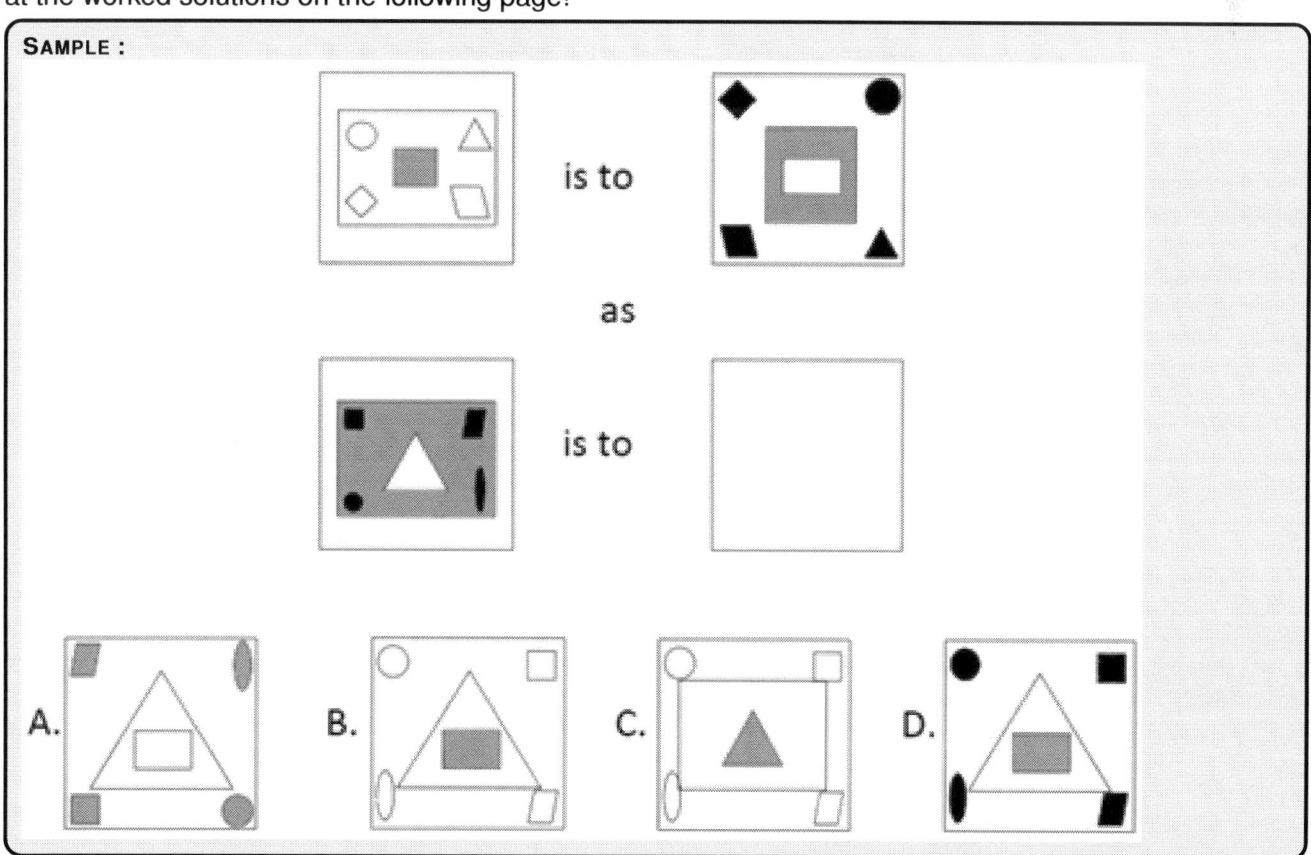

The first thing you may notice is how the four shapes in the corners of the big rectangle move outside the rectangle in the second image, and in doing so switch from white to black. So we can assume that the black corner shapes in the bottom image will turn white, hence eliminating options A and D. In addition, a particular corner shape is seen to move one space clockwise from the corner which it initially corresponded to. For instance, the circle in the top left corner moved outside of the rectangle to the top left corner of the outermost square and moved one space clockwise to the top right corner. This further reinforces that option A is incorrect, since the other alternatives have the correct positions for the corner shapes. Next, the larger white rectangle and the grey square in the middle switch places, so that the second image has a small white rectangle inside and on top of a larger grey square. This can then be applied to the bottom image, where the shape to complete the statement must have a smaller grey rectangle inside a larger white triangle, leading to the correct option B.

4.7 Strategy for type 4: *Pick Which Set* questions

The fourth question type in Abstract Reasoning is similar to the first question type for this section, since it involves two sets and calculating what crucial factor makes a square belong to either Set A or Set B. However, rather than having to pick whether a given Test Shape belongs to Set A, B, or Neither, you are now given four answer options each with their own square (which look like a 'Test Shape') and told to pick the option which belongs to Set A (or Set B, depending on what the question asks for). The strategy for this kind of question is pretty much the same as that for the first type, so let's just go through a couple of worked examples to increase your familiarity with this question type.

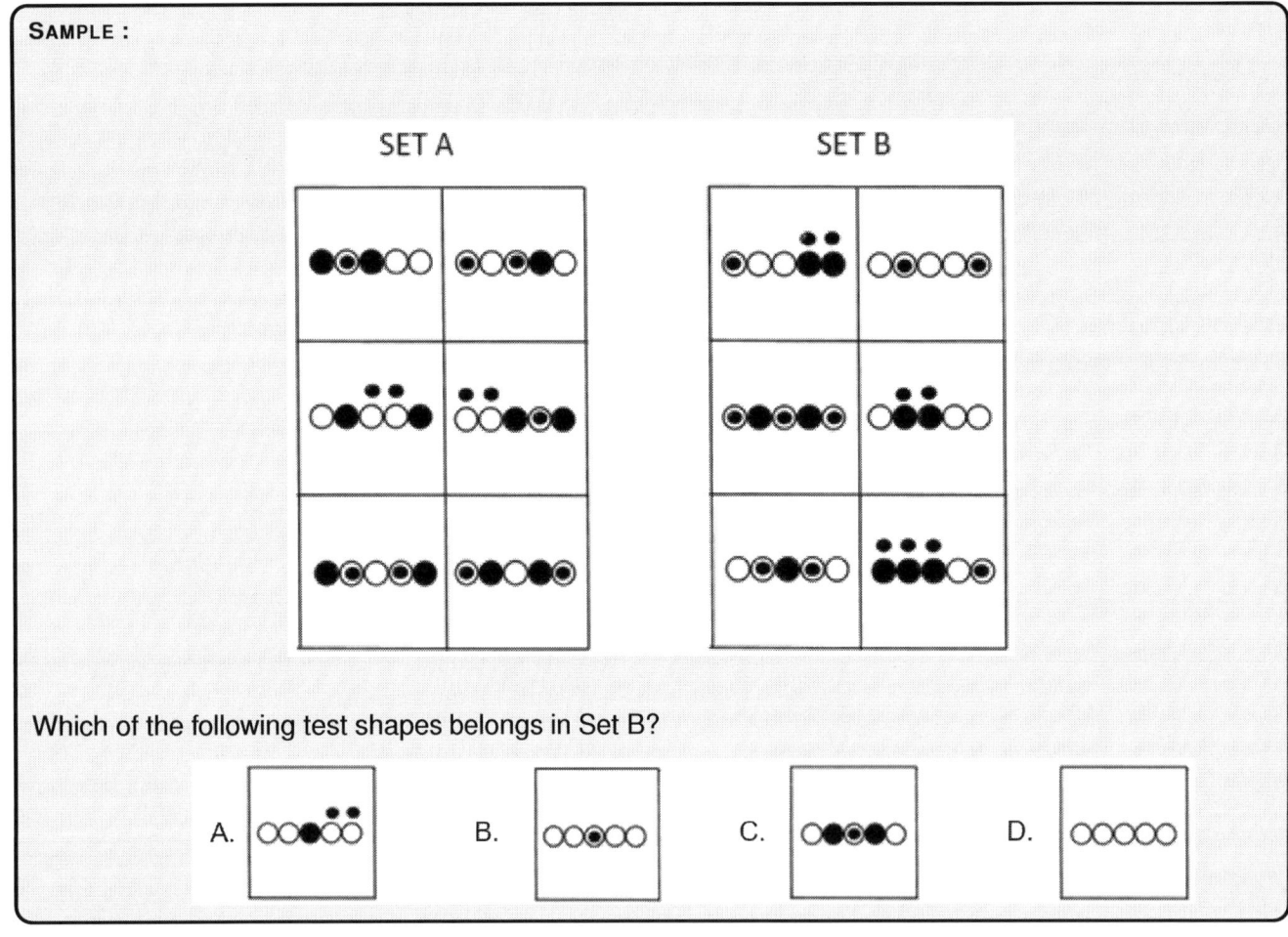

First of all, we can see that every single square in both Set A and Set B has five circles arranged in a row. Each of these squares involves at least one dot, either inside a circle or on top of it, and the position of this dot seems to have different effects in each of the sets – so we can assume that this is where the pattern lies. For Set A, the simplest square is the top left square, and here a dotted circle has a black circle on either side of it.

4.7 Strategy for type 4: Pick Which Set *questions*

We can compare this with the bottom right square, where the dotted circle is on either end of the row, with a black circle directly next to it and a white circle in the middle. This means that for Set A, wherever there is a dotted circle, the circles adjacent to it will be coloured black (we will call this Rule 1A). However, if we look at the top right square, only the circle to the right of the middle dotted circle is black. The circle which is common to both the leftmost dotted circle and the middle circle is white. So, from here, we can say that whenever there's a circle which is meant to be shaded black by two dotted circles simultaneously (i.e. a circle common to two dotted circles, or a circle in between two dotted circles) will become white (we will call this Rule 2A). This rule becomes even more evident when you look at the bottom left square, where the middle circle (between two dotted circles) is white and the rest are black.

To explain the circumstance of a dot being above a circle, let's look at the two middle squares. Whenever there is a dot above a circle, it appears in a pair and is never present alone. A black circle is on either side of the pair as well. So we can deduce that this occurs when two dotted circles are adjacent to each other, which causes the dots to go outside the circle and leave the original circle white (we will call this Rule 3A). However, Rule 2A does not seem to apply in Rule 3A, as seen in the middle right square, where a circle between two dotted circles (one is left with the dot inside and the other, originally dotted, now with the circle above it) is left black.

Considering that the array of **rules found in Set B are either similar or the opposite,** let us look at the top right square of this set. Here, either side of a dotted circle is white instead of black (we will call this Rule 1B). Move your attention to the middle left square, where the circle between two dotted circles are coloured black (we will call this Rule 2B). Both of these rules are seen in action in the bottom left square. Now, we can see that whenever there is a dot above a circle, it is found in a group of two or three, which is similar to Set A. So we can then also say that this occurs when two dotted circles are directly next to each other, and the circle under the dot is coloured black (we will call this rule 3B). However, this time, on either side of circles with a group of dots above it, it is left white, negating Rule 2B for this particular circumstance.

Looking at the options, we can instantly rule out option D, since a square must have at least one dot present anywhere, whether it be inside or outside a circle. In option C, the circles adjacent to the dotted circle are coloured black, which is a condition for Set A, so we can also eliminate this. In option A, the circles underneath the dots are white, which is a feature of Set A yet again, so this is eliminated. This then leaves option B, which meets all the criteria for Set B (where either side of a dotted circle is white).

SAMPLE :

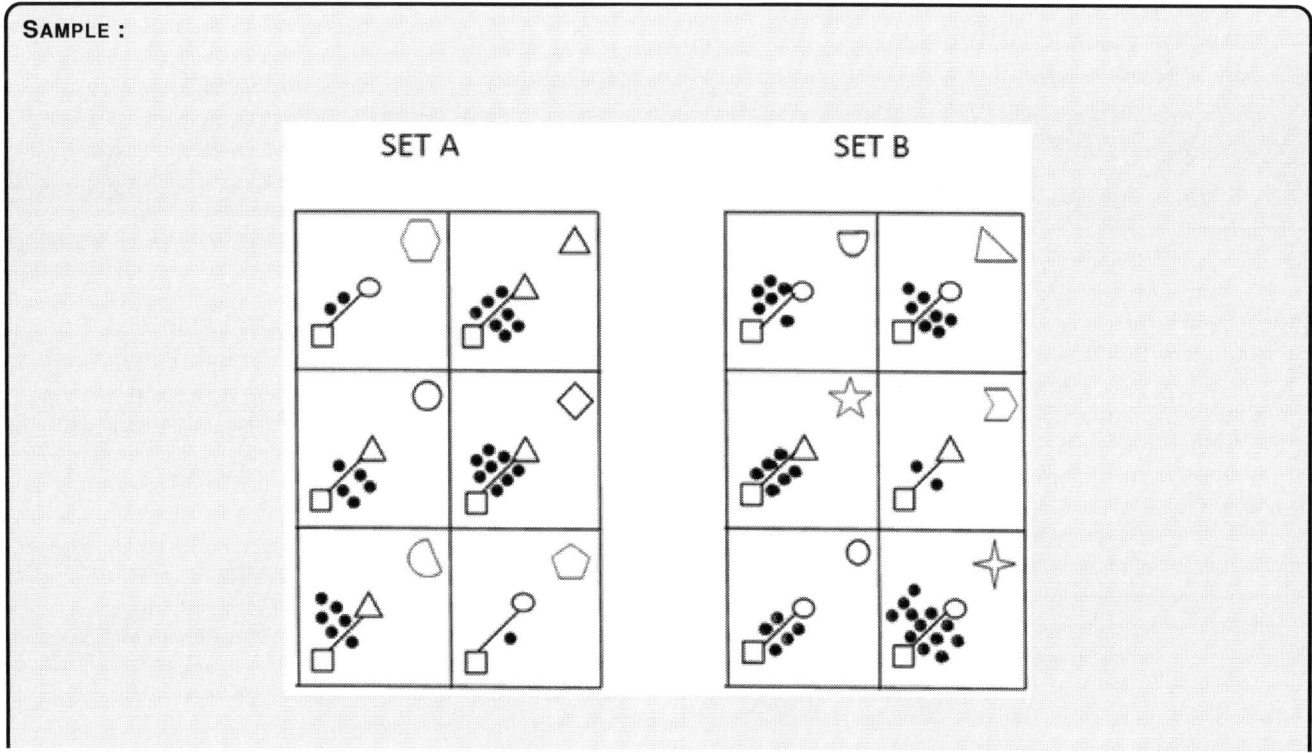

4.7 Strategy for type 4: Pick Which Set questions

Which of the following test shapes belongs in Set A?

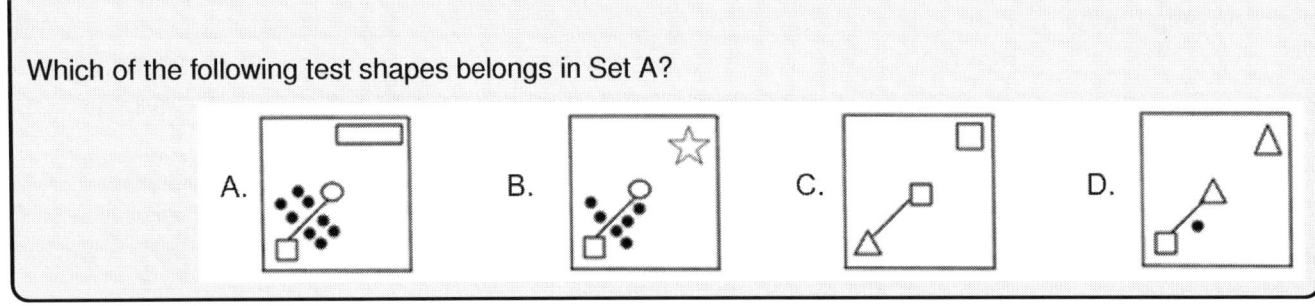

We can begin with the observation that all of the squares in Set A and Set B have a square in the bottom left corner which, via a line, is attached to either a circle or a triangle. In the top right corner of each square, there is a different regular shape, and on either side of the line that connects the square and the circle/triangle there is an arrangement of small black dots. Looking at Set A, you can see that there is a greater number of dots whenever the small square is attached to a triangle, and vice versa for a circle. Since the total number of shapes present, excluding the dots, remain the same, and the number of dots varies depending on the shape in the top right corner, we can look at the number of edges of the components. The middle right square has a diamond as its corner shape and a total of eight dots on either side of the line. One possible hypothesis is that the number of small black dots relates to the number of edges of the shapes present. Since eight is a sum of four and four, which is the number of edges for the corner square and the corner diamond, we can expand our hypothesis by saying that the number of edges of the corner shapes must be summed to give the number of black dots. This is further reinforced by the top right, middle left and bottom left squares of Set A. All of these have something in common: a triangle in the centre. Now, let's look at the top left square, which instead has a circle in the centre. The sum of the edges of the corner shapes is ten, but instead, we have only two dots. Nevertheless, two is the difference between the number of edges of the corner shapes (six from the hexagon and four from the square). So we can now say that for Set A, a triangle leads to the sum of the number of edges (Rule 1A) and a circle leads to the difference of the number of edges (Rule 2A).

For Set B, the opposite is found, where there is generally many more dots whenever a circle is in the centre. Since we know that the rules in Set B are often the opposite to those of Set A, we can test the hypothesis that a triangle leads to the difference of the number of edges in the corner shapes (Rule 1B) and a circle leads to the sum of the number of edges (Rule 2B). You can quickly test this by looking at the middle right square and the bottom left square because both of these squares are relatively simple.

A **distractor** in this question is the number of dots on either side of the line. What matters is the *total* number of black dots found in a square, and how many dots are on one specific side has no relationship to either of the set's rules. This supports the fact that you should start with testing out simpler rules before delving into more complex rules (such as whether there is a link between the number of dots on top of the line and the edges of the corner shapes), so that you do not waste precious time in the Abstract Reasoning section.

Now, let's go through the answer options. We can instantly eliminate option C since a square is not in the bottom left corner so it cannot belong to either set. For option A, there is a centre circle and the numbers of dots are the sum of the edges, which makes it belong to Set B instead of Set A. Option D has a centre triangle, and having one dot means that the triangle leads to a difference of the number of edges, which again falls under Set B. Option B, however, has a centre circle and there are six dots, which is the difference of the edges (ten from the star and four from the corner square), which is a condition of Set A.

4.8 Sample questions

SAMPLE:
Questions 1–4

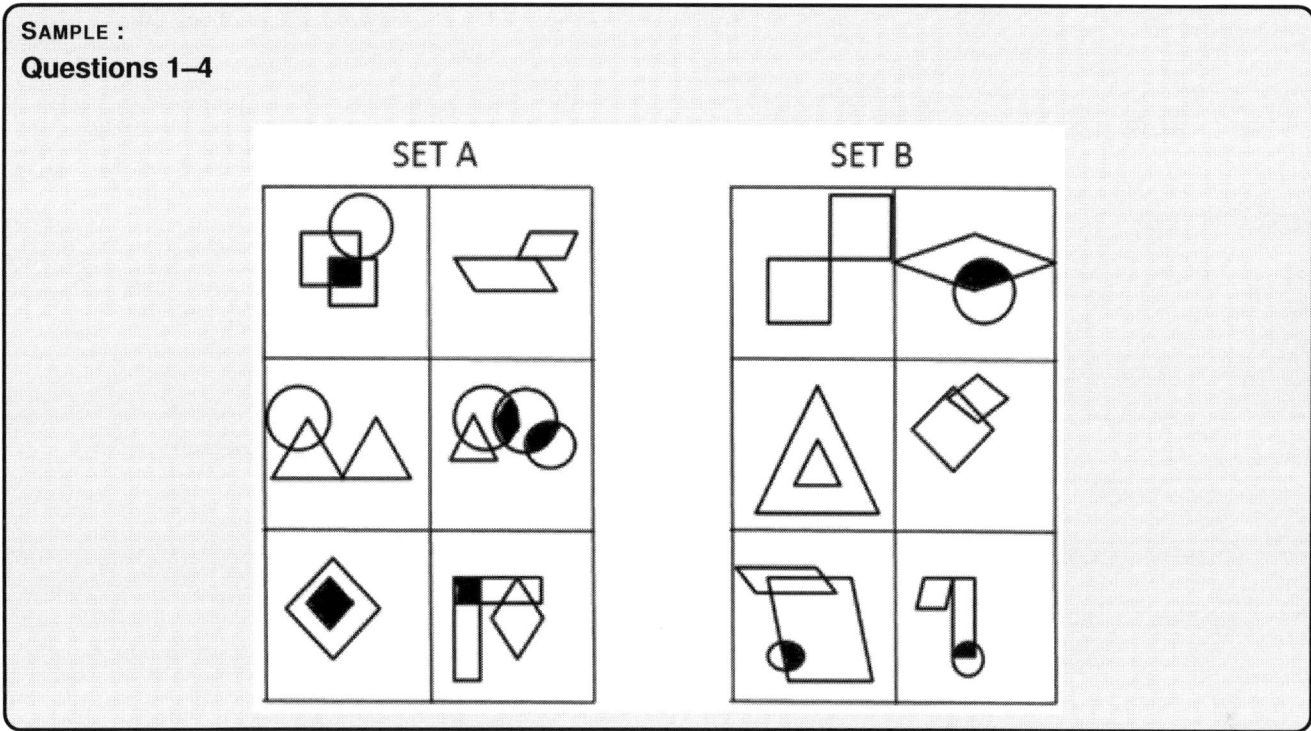

Question 1

TEST SHAPE

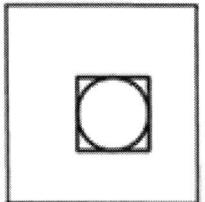

1. Set A
2. Set B
3. Neither

Question 2

TEST SHAPE

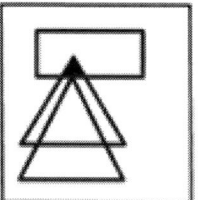

1. Set A
2. Set B
3. Neither

Question 3

TEST SHAPE

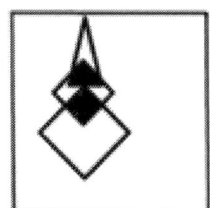

1. Set A
2. Set B
3. Neither

Question 4

TEST SHAPE

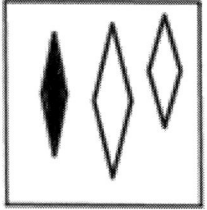

1. Set A
2. Set B
3. Neither

4.8 Sample questions

SAMPLE :
Question 5

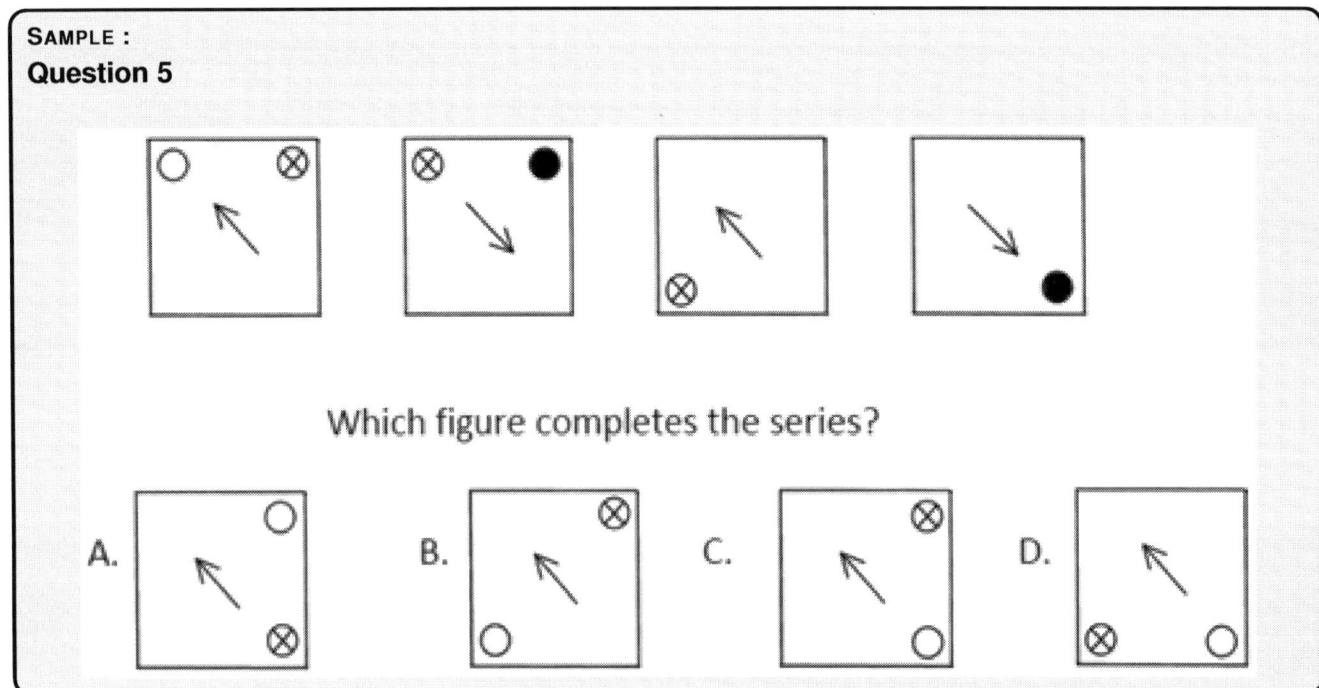

SAMPLE :
Question 6

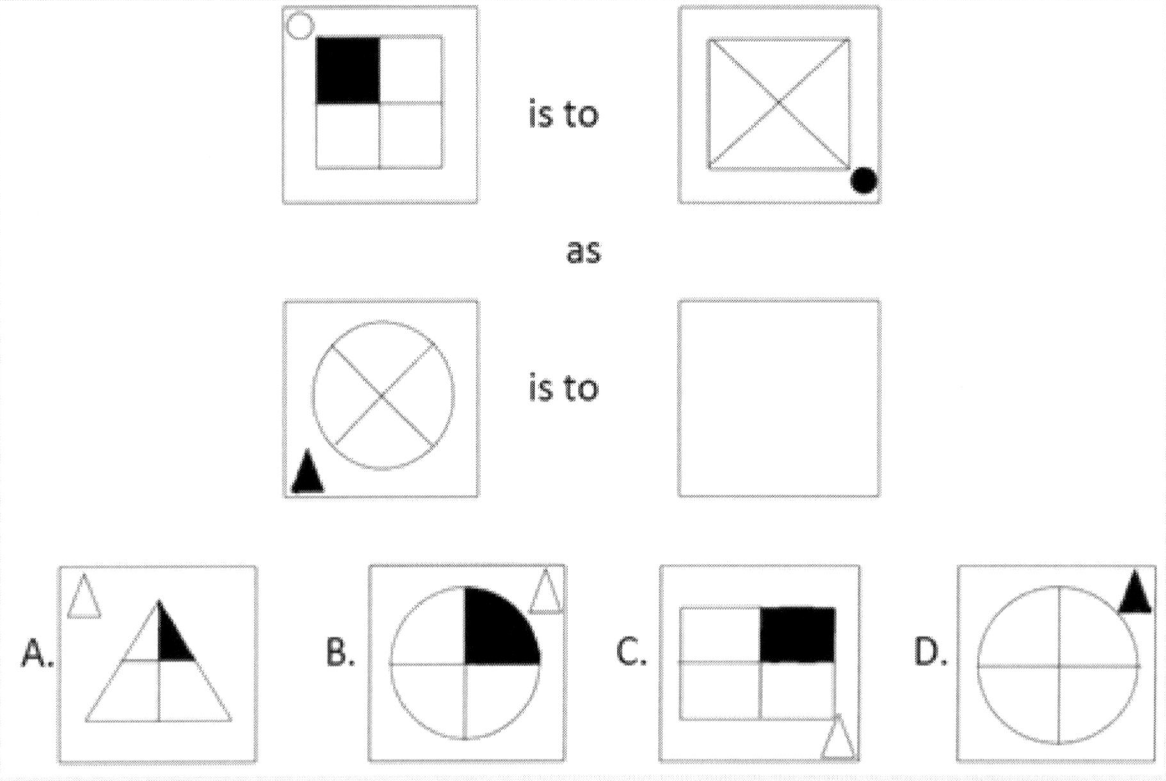

4.8 Sample questions

SAMPLE:
Question 7

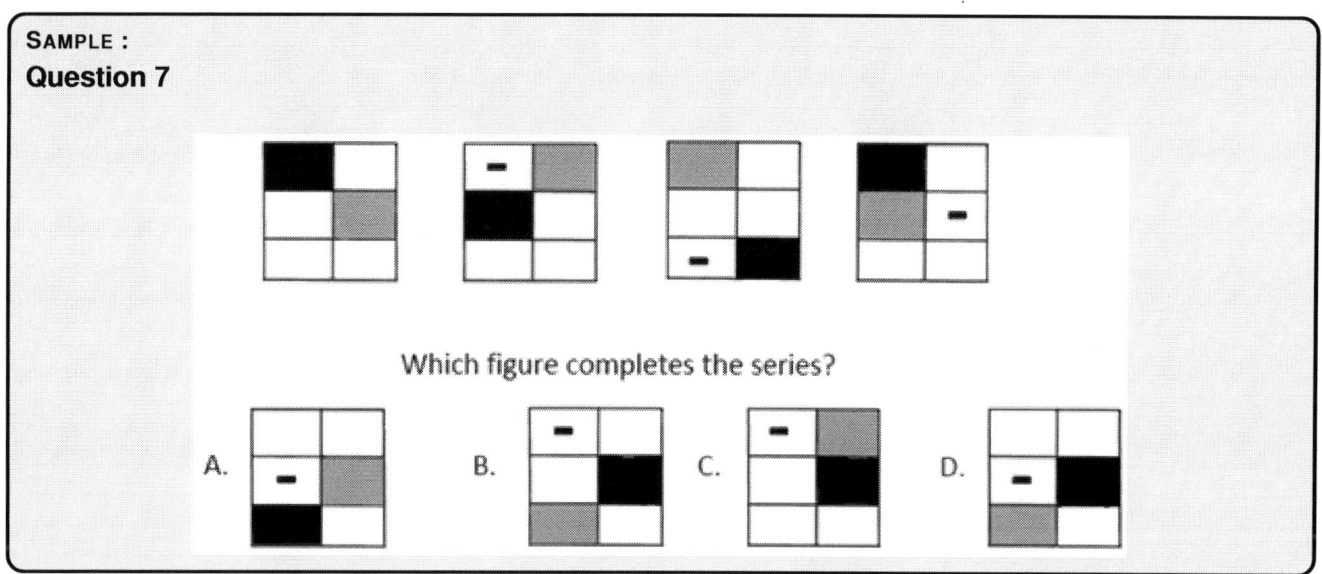

Which figure completes the series?

A. B. C. D.

SAMPLE:
Question 8

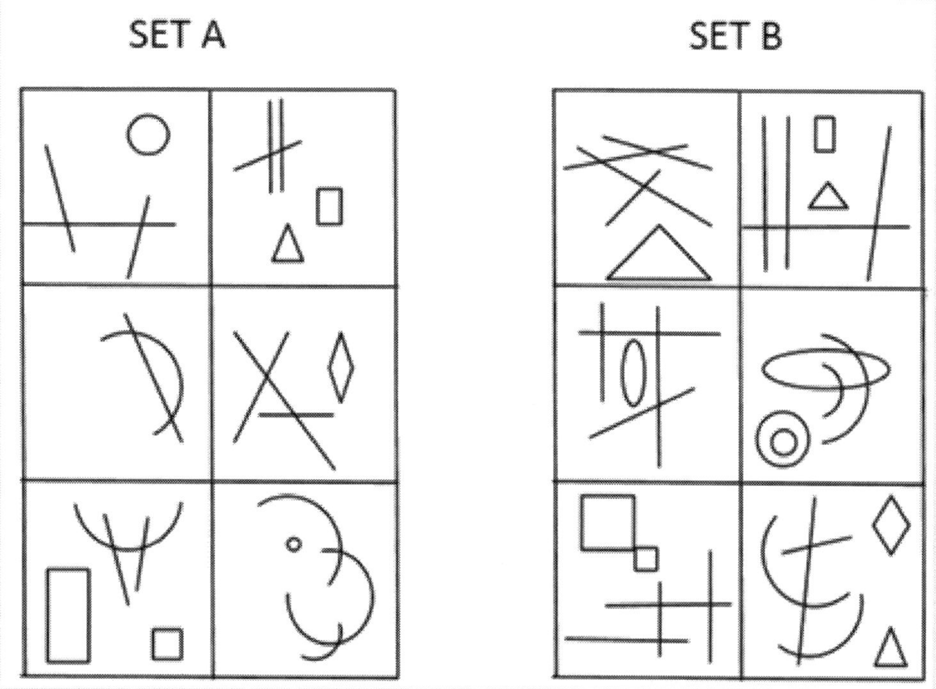

SET A   SET B

Which of the following test shapes belongs in Set B?

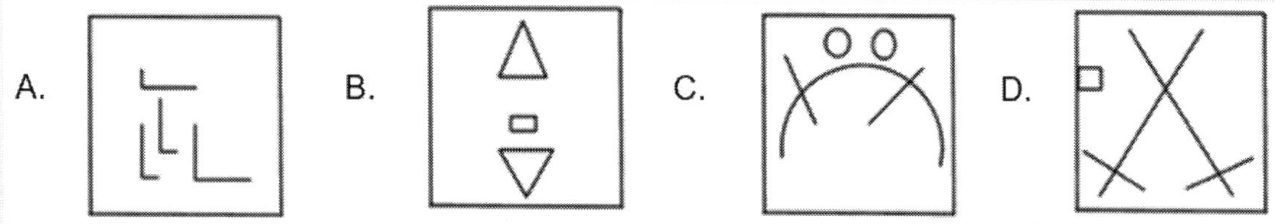

A. B. C. D.

Section 4 – Abstract Reasoning

4.8 Sample questions

SAMPLE:
Question 9

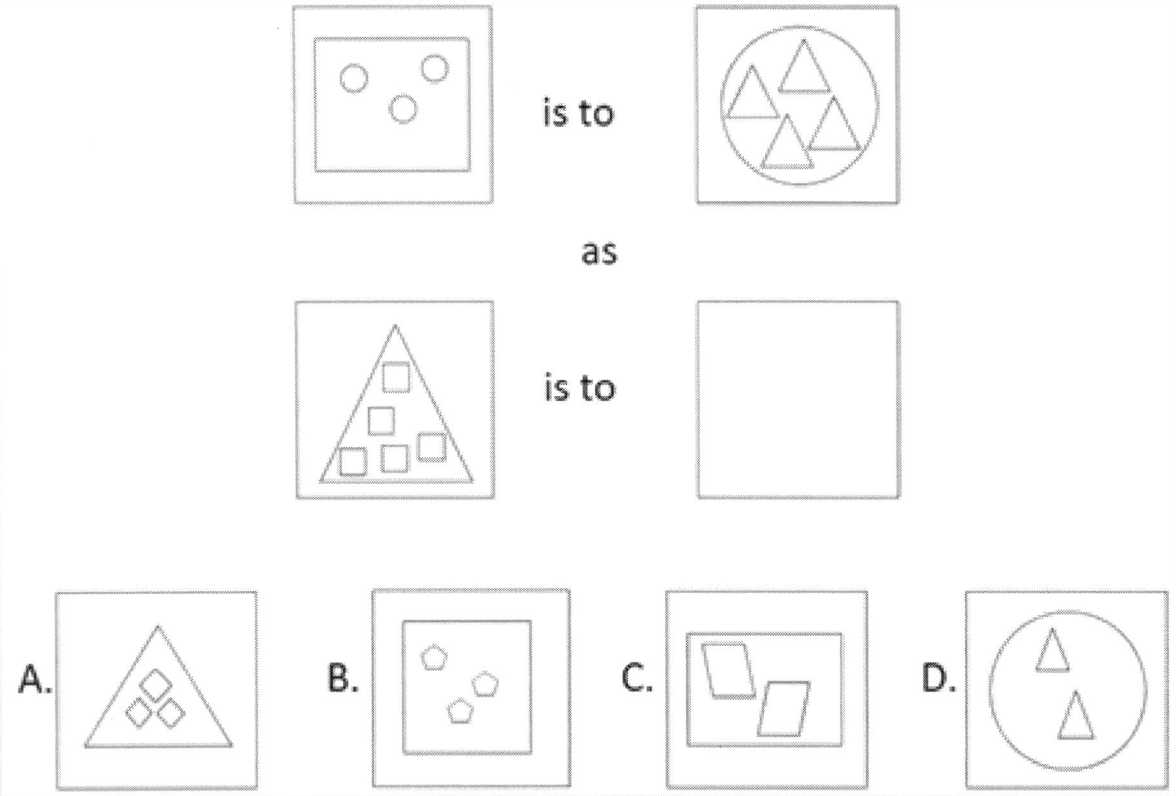

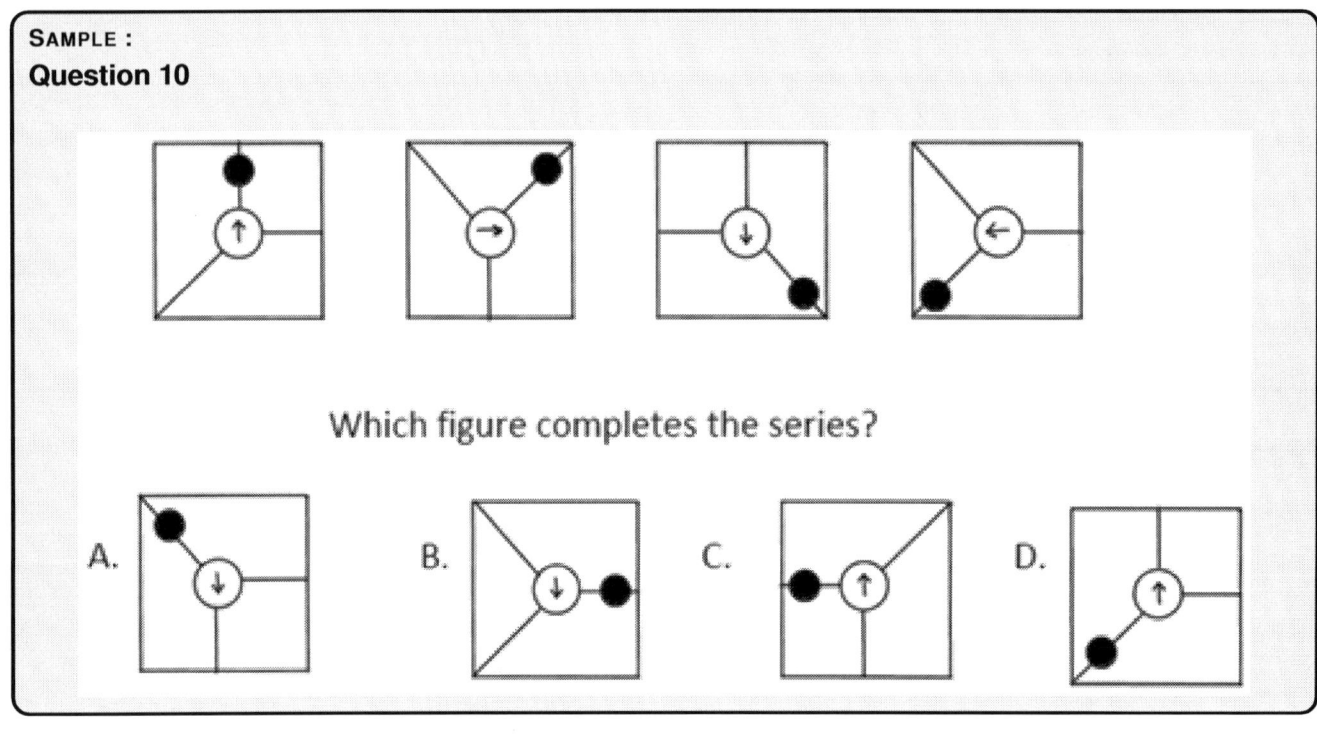

SAMPLE:
Question 10

Which figure completes the series?

4.9 Answers to sample questions

Question 1: A

For a shape to belong to Set A, it must adhere to the following set of rules:

- Shapes of the same type which overlap have the overlapped region coloured.
- Shapes of different types which overlap do not have the overlapped region coloured.

For a shape to belong to Set B, it must adhere to the following set of rules:

- Shapes of the same type which overlap do not have the overlapped region coloured.
- Shapes of different types which overlap have the overlapped region coloured.

Here, the test shape has two components of different shape types overlapping, with a circle inside a square, and the overlapped region is not coloured. Therefore, it meets the condition of Set A.

Question 2: B

For this question, the test shape has two components of different shape types overlapping (a triangle and a rectangle) and the overlapped region is coloured. Along with this, the triangle also overlaps with another triangle, which is of the same shape type, and the overlapped region is not coloured. These make the test shape meet the criteria for Set B. Hence the answer is B.

Question 3: C

In this question, the test shape has two components of different shape types overlapping (a triangle and a diamond) and the overlapped region is coloured. However, the diamond also overlaps with another diamond, which is of the same shape type, and the overlapped region is coloured. These conflict with the criteria to belong to either Set A or B. Hence the answer is C, Neither.

Question 4: C

As shown in this question, the test shape involves three components of the same type (a long diamond) and none of these shapes overlap with each other. However, one of these diamonds are coloured anyway, and this characteristic conflicts with the criteria needed to belong to either Set A or Set B. Hence the answer is C, Neither.

Question 5: C

The arrow in the centre of the squares alternate between pointing to the top left corner and the bottom right corner, so in the fifth square, it should point to the top left corner. This does not eliminate any alternatives since all answer options have the arrow pointing to the top left.

The circle with the cross in it (let's call it the 'cross circle') starts from the top right corner, then moves one corner anti-clockwise for each square along. This means that it should finally be in the top right corner again in the fifth square. Note that it is covered by the black circle in the fourth square. This then eliminates answer options A and D.

The remaining circle is white in the first square, but is then black in the second and fourth squares, so we can assume that it alternates between being white and black, meaning that it should be white next in the series (though this does not help with elimination). It moves by one space clockwise then disappears in the third square, but we can assume that it is hiding behind the cross circle. Therefore, this component follows the 1-2-3-4 rule, where the fifth square should have the white circle being in the bottom right corner. Hence, the answer is C.

4.9 Answers to sample questions

Question 6: B

Firstly, what can be observed is that there is one shape in a corner outside of a larger shape, which is either criss-crossed horizontally and vertically or diagonally, and only one component is shaded black in a single square. From the first pair, the small white circle on the outside moves to its opposite corner from the top left to the bottom right. The criss-cross pattern has also alternated from horizontal/vertical to diagonal (or you could also say that the four lines inside the large square have rotated clockwise or anti-clockwise by $45°$).

The component which is shaded black is switched from the segment of the large square (which corresponds to the circle or is closest to it) to the outer circle. From here, we can assume that the small black triangle in the bottom pair will be positioned in the top right corner (eliminating options A and C) and will be white instead. This immediately leads to the correct answer of option B, but we will confirm the other patterns as well.

The large circle must also remain as the large shape inside the square and will now have a horizontal/vertical criss-cross pattern instead of a diagonal one, which is only seen in options B and D. Finally, the segment of the circle which corresponds to the outer triangle must now be coloured black. Hence the answer is option B.

Question 7: B

The patterns for this set are:

- The black space moves via the 1-2-3-4 rule anti-clockwise around the six spaces (so must now be in the middle right space, eliminating option A).
- The grey space moves one space anti-clockwise (so must now be in the bottom left space, eliminating option C).
- The small black rectangle moves two spaces anti-clockwise, hiding behind the grey space in the first square (so must now be in the top left space, eliminating option D).

Hence the answer is B.

Question 8: D

For this question, it is all too easy to get overwhelmed by the seemingly random arrangement of components, so try to zoom out a little and view both sets with a bird's eye perspective. You will see that in every single square for both sets, there is always a group of lines that intersect regardless of whether there is another shape within the square or not. So, for now, we can identify that the presence of the closed shapes are a distractor. Looking at Set A, you will notice that there are only two points of intersection between any two or three lines, thus this is the rule which sets apart squares that belong to this set. Now assessing Set B, the rule is similar to that of Set A in that there are only three points of intersection within a group of lines for a single square.

Keeping this in mind, we can now look at the answer options. Option A does not have any points of intersection, so it does not belong to either set. You may argue that each of the four components are two lines meeting, but the given sets demonstrate that the intersections must be clear, so the lines cannot just touch each other. Option B only has regular shapes, which is irrelevant and only acts as a distractor, hence it can be eliminated. Option C has three lines with two points of intersection, which is a feature of Set A. This leaves Option D, which indeed contains three points of intersection, making it belong to Set B. Hence the answer is D.

Question 9: B

This question involves a trickier set of patterns amongst its components. The first thing that should stand out to you is that no colouration is involved, neither in the question stem nor in the given alternatives. If we were to follow the acronym SCANS, we will start with 'Shape' and observe that all of the components involved are regular shapes and there is no pattern with open or closed shapes. Skipping 'Colour', we can look at the 'Arrangement' of the components, which actually seems random. No angles are being used, nothing is being rotated, it does not seem to matter if a smaller shape meets the corners of the larger shape or not, none of the shapes overlap and nothing is being mirrored. Let us then look at 'Number', where we can note down the number of the components involved and the number of edges they have. You would then notice the following:

- **Top left square:** number of sides of larger shape = 4, amount of smaller shapes = 3, number of sides of smaller shape = 1
- **Top right square:** number of sides of larger shape = 1, amount of smaller shapes = 4, number of sides of smaller shape = 3)

A clear relationship is evident between the above numbers. In the second square of a pair, the number of sides of the larger shape equal to the number of sides of the smaller shape in the first square. The amount of smaller shapes in the second square is equal to the number of sides of the larger shape in the first square. Finally, the number of sides of the smaller shape in the second square equals to the amount of smaller shapes in the first square. To make this relationship clearer to you, try drawing arrows between each of these figures, as shown below. Notice that I have used shorthand to describe the components' rules, which will save you a lot of time especially with harder or more confusing questions.

Square A ---> Square B
#sides (large shape)
(small shapes)
#sides (small shape)

Apply these overarching set of rules to the bottom pair and you get the following:

- **Bottom left square:** # sides (large shape) = 3, # (small shapes) = 5, #sides (small shape) = 4
- **Bottom right square:** #sides (large shape) = 4, # (small shapes) = 3, #sides (small shape) = 5

Therefore, the final answer must have a four-sided larger shape (eliminating options A and D) and three five-sided shapes or pentagons. Hence the answer is option B.

Question 10: C

The patterns for this set are:

- The arrow inside the centre circle rotates clockwise by 90° (so must now be pointing up, eliminating options A and B).
- Each of the lines around the circle moves around anti-clockwise by 45° (i.e. the line going upwards in the first square must now be going downwards, the line going right in the first square must now be going left; and the line joining the circle to the bottom left corner must now be joining the circle with the top right corner – this alone gives you the answer C). To help you identify this pattern, which is quite tricky to detect at first, you should focus on the move of a single line in the series and then check, one at a time, if the other lines are following suit in the same manner. You can differentiate the three lines by marking them distinctly, such as drawing a cross at the end of the line which points upwards in the first square and drawing the same cross for the same line in the rest of the squares – then drawing different 'markers' for the other two lines.
- An even trickier pattern to detect is the movement of the black circle. This circle is dependent on the lines and moves to the line on its right in the following square, travelling clockwise in the series (so must now be on the line pointing to the left from the circle).

Hence, the answer is C.

Section 5

Section 5 – Situation Judgement Test

5.1 Introduction

The final component of the UCAT is called the Situational Judgement Test. This also happens to be a separate exam and selection criterion in its own right for postgraduate entrance into Monash Medicine via the Biomedical Science pathway, and is a highly important consideration for prospective medical students. In the UCAT, this section starts with one minute to read the instructions, and then 26 minutes to take the test and attempt to answer all 69 questions.

This section assesses your ability to **understand situations and conflicts** that occur in the real world and their capacity to identify significant aspects of the situation and the **appropriate course of action to take** in order to deal with it. In other words, this section looks at your level of **ethical conduct** (such as your consideration of informed consent), your **decision-making skills in a stressful environment** and your **professionalism.**

The majority of these scenarios will be **health-based** – for example, questions may involve a medical student working under a consultant at a hospital, or ethical dilemmas that are likely to be experienced in a clinical setting.

The Situational Judgement Test measures a variety of essential attributes in a prospective medical student, such as **team coordination** or involvement, **empathising** with different perspectives, **endurance/resilience, integrity,** and the ability to **adapt.** Unlike the other UCAT sections, which tend to be more objective in their answers and are more academic in nature, this component judges your own perceptions and line of thinking by throwing you into real-life scenarios and directly asking you about the **quality of different possible responses.**

A few examples of real-life situations which the exam's questions may be based around include:

- Handling a loud roommate
- Dealing with a friend who plagiarised in an assessment task
- A patient bringing up controversial research that may affect their health decisions (such as vaccinating their children, or undergoing unsafe elective surgery)
- Navigating a conversation with a colleague who is insecure about their performance at work
- Talking to a patient's family who are having disagreements about treatment options

Whilst the questions are usually set in the medical field, they do not require knowledge about specific medical procedures. Situational Judgement Tests are widely used in any form of medical selection, including those for general practitioners as well as other medical speciality fields.

In this fifth section of the UCAT, you will have to read through 22 scenarios with between 2 and 5 questions each, leading to a grand total of 69 questions. With 26 minutes of test-taking time, this gives you around 23 seconds on average to answer each question, so this section is similar to the the Abstract Reasoning section in terms of time pressure. For a given scenario, you will be provided with a statement for each question (e.g. if a scenario has five questions under it, each question will have a separate statement) and you are required to judge it using the list of answer options provided.

One of the question types involves rating a given factor's importance to the scenario's conflict from four options (such as 'Very important', 'Important', 'Of minor importance,' or 'Not important at all'). The other type of question asks you to pick the most or least appropriate response to the scenario from a list of three courses of action given to you in the options; however, this type of question is not as common as the multiple-choice question type (where you rate the appropriateness or importance of a given response). A drag-and-drop interface can be utilised in this UCAT section, although the majority of Situational Judgement Test questions will be multiple-choice with four answer options.

5.2 Core skills

5.2.1 Reading proficiency and speed reading

While the passages are not as long as those in the Verbal Reasoning section, they are by no means short either! Having an ability to speed read will prove highly useful for this section, though it is fine if you find yourself not being able to read your highest possible speed because your priority should be your level of **understanding of the text.** In other words, it will not be of help if you rapidly read through a passage but recall nothing, as this just means you will need to read the text over and over again. This often just results in more time being wasted than if you were to read the transcript at a normal, comfortable pace and get a good grasp of what is happening right from the start, thus enabling you to answer the questions much faster. For specific tips on how to work on your speed reading skills, see page 5.

5.2.2 Empathy and compromise

It is important to be able to put yourself in the shoes of people who are involved in the scenario since doing so helps with identifying the core issues that a particular situation deals with. For example, if a scenario is about a doctor forcing a patient who is a Jehovah's Witness to get a blood transfusion, empathising with the patient can help you identify that this situation deals with issues surrounding patient autonomy and medical paternalism (don't worry if you don't know what these mean yet; we'll explore these concepts later!).

However, due to the nature of SJT questions, you must maintain a degree of objectivity so that you can judge a given action in an impartial way. As we will explore in this chapter, when rating how 'appropriate' someone's response is, we need to consider how **morally right** the action is, rather than whether it 'makes sense' for the person to take that action.

For instance, suppose a scenario involves two research colleagues working under the same supervisor and someone (let's call them Petyr) plagiarises a significant portion of a scientific paper for their PhD out of desperation. Petyr is under a lot of pressure at home, has two other jobs, and has three kids to look after – hence, he has very little time to write a particular section of the PhD himself. They ask their colleague (let's call them Rebecca) not to tell anyone else. You are asked to rate the appropriateness of Rebecca's potential response: 'Report Petyr to her supervisor.' You may be tempted to say this is 'A very inappropriate thing to do,' considering that it would add another source of pressure to Petyr, who is already heavily stressed and Petyr specifically told Rebecca to not tell on him. However, you must keep in mind that plagiarism is a violation of academic integrity, and a very serious matter when it comes something as significant as a PhD. The correct answer would actually be 'Inappropriate, but not awful' because dealing with misconduct like plagiarism is one of a supervisor's duties. However, reporting to a supervisor is not an appropriate first step, or immediate go-to option. It's often best to try and resolve problems amongst the people involved wherever possible, rather than always escalating situations to one's superiors (i.e. if the scenario involved Petyr being jealous or irritable towards Rebecca, then Rebecca immediately going to her Head of Department, or the Chancellor of the University would be *very inappropriate!*) so Rebecca should discuss with Petyr the consequences of plagiarism, and then try to help him wherever she can (such as, if they're close, looking after Petyr's children for a day while Petyr spends that time on his PhD).

5.3 General advice for Section 5

The Situational Judgement test is the final section of the UCAT, but you still need to sustain your full concentration during this section. A common mistake students make is to 'burn out' by putting an extreme amount of effort into the Verbal Reasoning and Decision-Making sections, only to have their focus gradually decrease until their capacity to answer the Situational Judgement Test questions is significantly impeded. Though universities can differ in the way they interpret UCAT results, many institutions in the United Kingdom do not accept applicants who score poorly in the SJT section, despite earning high marks in the other four sections, because of how critically important situational judgement is in the medical field.

5.3 General advice for Section 5

Treat the UCAT exam as a **marathon** rather than a set of five separate short sprints. You need to pace yourself and excel in every single sub-test, including the Situational Judgement Test, with a similarly high level of attention to maximise your chances at a competitive mark for all the universities you apply to.

In terms of approaching each question, you must **read the whole scenario first,** and ensure you thoroughly understand what is happening in the situation before you start to answer the given questions. A general guideline to follow, in terms of the time you should aim to take, is to allocate **30 seconds to comprehensively read the scenario** and develop an understanding of the premise behind it and **10 seconds to answer each of the related questions.** Before moving on to the questions, you can give yourself a little bit more time to consider the general dilemmas which the situation contains, such as whether it deals with issues of confidentiality, dishonesty, integrity, etc. It is okay if you cannot meet these time limits at first because your level of understanding is what needs to be prioritised over how quickly you can get through a particular set of questions. You are more likely to end up with a higher score if you fully comprehend and thus confidently answer 90% of the questions, rather than race through and make flawed or educated guesses about 100% of them.

5.3.1 Judging appropriateness

It is worth noting that for a particular scenario, certain options may appear or ratings can appear in multiple questions. A misconception some candidates may have is that once a certain option has been chosen for a question, such as 'A very inappropriate thing to do,' this option cannot be chosen again for any of the following questions under the same scenario, even though it may seem like the correct answer to give. Do not mistake the options as a word bank, where you cross off one answer option after using it! It is actually quite common that a handful of the questions for one scenario will have the same rating as the most correct answer. Although rare, there is also a chance that every single question has the same option as the correct answer, such as 'A very appropriate thing to do'. These options are not mutually exclusive, as **there can be more than one 'very appropriate' or 'very inappropriate' response** to a situation.

Similarly, another important thing to keep in mind is that the answer options provided to you are not intended to represent all possible courses of action to solve the dilemma in the scenario at hand. In other words, the action you think would have been the most appropriate or important may not be present amongst the options. However, you must not let this affect your judgement of the given response. Whilst you may be able to think of a potential response that is 'A very appropriate thing to do,' do not let this influence your perception of the provided responses (where, for example, you might be tempted to give one of the answer options a lower rating because you have thought of your own more appropriate/important factor), since they may also be 'A very appropriate thing to do' except in a different way. To illustrate this, let's go through a worked example below.

> **SAMPLE:**
> Jessica is a third-year medical student who has been asked to supervise a patient with an infection that can get worse at any minute. This supervision has been allocated to her at the very last minute and put in a slot where she is meant to have a break when she had planned to check on her best friend, Stella, who is suffering from a serious heart issue. After being in the room for four hours and seeing that there is no sign that the condition of the patient, who is now quietly reading a book, is getting worse, she suddenly gets a phone call from Stella's mum who says that Stella had a heart attack and is currently in a critical condition. Jessica becomes anxious and really wants to go and be there for her dear friend.
>
> How **appropriate** are each of the following responses by **Jessica** in this situation?
>
> **Question 1:** Explain the situation to the patient and immediately leave to see Stella.
>
> (a) A very appropriate thing to do
> (b) Appropriate, but not ideal
> (c) Inappropriate, but not awful
> (d) A very inappropriate thing to do

The correct answer here is option D. Even though the given response is better than Jessica simply abandoning the patient without giving them an explanation, it is still a very inappropriate action to take. This is especially true considering that Jessica knows the patient's condition could get worse at any minute, so while they may be perfectly fine now, they could potentially rapidly deteriorate the minute she leaves the room. This would demonstrate Jessica's disregard to her duty of care as a medical student, and if this patient were to die, Jessica could be held responsible because she should have been able to notify the patient's doctor if she had been in the room, hence potentially preventing their death.

Getting back to the core of this question, you may have considered giving Jessica's response the rating 'Inappropriate, but not awful' due to it being not as terrible as the hypothetical scenario of not notifying the patient at all. But both responses are equally 'very inappropriate' since they both mean that a patient's life is gravely endangered and Jessica is neglecting her responsibilities.

Again, just like with Abstract Reasoning and the previous sections, putting in a lot of practice makes a significant difference. Practise Situational Judgement Test questions as much as you can, ranging from those provided on the official UCAT website to free online questions provided by different companies and forums. This will increase your familiarity with these types of questions and help you solidify your approach in judging different kinds of responses (e.g. gaining informed consent from the patient for a crucial medical decision is almost always 'A very appropriate thing to do'). By exposing yourself to a large variety of ethical dilemmas, whether it is in the medical context or not, you will greatly increase your confidence and abilities in dealing with the scenarios that will be given to you in the real exam.

5.3.2 Practice log of ethical issues

During your practice, you will be exposed to a very wide range of scenarios and real-life ethical dilemmas, so you should keep a small list or table of all the qualities or principles that were tested in each of these scenarios. Ideally, you should also keep track of which ones appear in multiple scenarios, as this can help you identify particularly common concerns that you are likely to see in the UCAT itself. For an example of what this may look like, refer to the table below.

Principle/quality/concept/issue	Tested more than one time?
Maintain public confidence in Medicine (e.g. don't demean a medical professional in front of other patients).	YES
It's always appropriate to apologise to patients for a long wait, regardless of the reason and regardless of how the patient behaves (whether they're nice or not).	
Informed consent (e.g. a patient who has sufficient mental and physical capacity should still always be involved in decisions regarding their treatment and follow-up care). This is really important, even if the medical team disagree with the patient's perspective about the treatment plan.	
Don't jump to conclusions.	YES
Patients have a right to autonomy.	YES
Ensure that the patient has a full understanding of what the doctor is saying and what their treatment will contain (e.g. through simple diagrams that the doctor draws) and that the doctor has a full understanding of what the patient is saying (rather than dismissing their opinion since they're the doctor).	YES

5.3 General advice for Section 5

Address a problem when you know you're capable of doing so, rather than leaving it unaddressed (since it will make things inefficient and troublesome for you and others). Resolve the issue at hand instead of just 'putting up with it.'	YES
Be professional (e.g. be polite, don't swear or using demeaning language, respect boundaries and cultures).	YES
Be honest and firm when telling someone else, such as a patient, about a problem they have caused which is bothering staff and other patients (e.g. too much noise).	
Don't be confrontational when it's not necessary and don't be accusatory.	YES
Keep a balance between sympathy and pragmatism, such as when giving advice to someone in a critical condition or palliative care.	
Don't waste time when something is urgent.	
Respect policies and rules of establishments (e.g. university academic rules, hospital regulations and codes of conduct).	
Ensure public safety (first priority is patient health and safety, followed by patient comfort, and then public confidence).	
Own up to your mistakes (e.g. your colleagues' opinions of you shouldn't matter), and consider the causes of your mistake to prevent them from happening again.	YES
Negotiate conflicts with patients (be reasonable, assess how worthwhile each person's contributions are, draw from prior experience, consider whose knowledge may be based on outdated information rather than up-to-date data, etc.).	YES
Allocate equal work in a project to all team members; be fair and ensure equity.	
If you have at least some knowledge on how to deal with an emergency, where there's no one with greater expertise currently at hand (e.g. you know most, but not all steps of CPR, and a person has gone into cardiac arrest), you should take action. Even though you don't know the full procedure, it's better you have tried rather than doing nothing at all.	
Always maintain patient confidentiality.	
Address problems immediately, but look for local, lower-tier help before escalating the situation and going to a superior (i.e. talk to the person directly involved in the problem first).	
Seek advice from people who are senior and with greater experience in a certain field.	
Illegal acts and blatantly lying are always 'very inappropriate.'	
Do not apologise on behalf of another person (they should take responsibility rather than having someone else solve their problem for them). Be accountable for your own actions, but not for the actions of others.	
Report inappropriate or illegal behaviour yourself.	
Doctors must try to support their patients' wishes.	

Along with listing the main principles, you may also want to add in reasons why you got some questions wrong and what the rationale behind the correct answer was. Having a read over the **Good Medical Practice guidelines** published by the General Medical Council will also help you build this bank of principles since it details what it takes to be considered a good doctor. These guidelines are available at: https://www.gmc-uk.org/ethical-guidance/ethical-guidance-for-doctors.

5.3.3 Medical ethics terminology

While preparing for this section, you may come across terms such as 'patient confidentiality' and 'patient autonomy' and not know what they mean. Below is a table consisting of the descriptions of each of these common phrases which can be potential issues that a question can encompass. We will also revisit these when discussing advice for your interviews, so it's good to familiarise yourself with these now! You are not expected to know these definitions off by heart, since medical knowledge is not required for the UCAT, but it will be helpful to get an idea of these concepts to guide your decisions in the Situational Judgement Test.

Term	Description
Patient autonomy	When deemed **competent,** patients must have a say when it comes to decisions regarding their health. Doctors must avoid forcing patients to do something regarding their health; rather, a decision must be made by the patient themselves. A patient can be judged **incompetent** if they are very young, unconscious, confused and frail, or impaired mentally (e.g. intoxication, dementia). In this case, it is up to their guardian and the doctor to make the decisions for them.
Informed consent	When deemed competent, patients have a right to fully understand what a certain medical procedure involves, then provide their **permission** for it. Characteristics for competency and incompetency are the same as those listed under patient autonomy.
Patient confidentiality	Medical professionals must respect their patients' **privacy,** restricting public access to the health records and other information of patients. Some examples include taking out a patient's name and other identifying details when educating medical students, and not talking about patient cases in a public area, like an elevator or public transport.
Medical paternalism	This relates to a doctor **overriding the preferences** of a patient when the doctor believes it is in the best interest of the patient to do so. Examples of this include insisting a vegan patient with iron deficiencies eat red meat, or demanding a fasting Muslim patient drink water before a blood test. Medical paternalism is generally **unjustified** and looked down upon because contemporary medical practice is based on patient autonomy where patients have a legal and ethical right to be involved in decisions regarding their treatment.
Public confidence in medicine	This describes the public's trust in doctors and health practitioners. It is important that the public know they are safe in the hands of dignified and skilled professionals who act in the best interests of their patients. To maintain this faith, health practitioners must act in a professional manner at all times during their work (such as not talking on the phone during a consultation or reprimanding another doctor in front of their patient).

5.3.4 Assessing perspectives

As a general rule, you must ensure that you read all questions correctly, but further to this, in the Situational Judgement Test, you must make sure that you provide an answer from the perspective of the correct individual (as identified in the stem of the question). This is because the rating for appropriateness of a response may change depending on who the question is talking about, as in the below example.

> **SAMPLE:**
> Two best friends, Joey and Kyle, attend the same school. They were friends since first grade and Kyle knows Joey to be a very extroverted and confident person. However, in the last month, Kyle noticed that he's been a bit distant and has been skipping third period on Thursdays increasingly often until he stopped going to it completely. Kyle finally confronts him about it, and eventually, Joey tells him that he feels that the new Japanese teacher hates him. This teacher not only gives him lower marks when the quality of his answers is the same as the classmates who scored highly but also ignores him when he puts his hands up in class and ridicules him when he asks a question after class. Recently, the teacher escalated to calling him racist slurs under his breath. Joey tried telling the teacher that he didn't appreciate what he said and did, but the teacher denied being offensive and brushed him off. He then tells Kyle not to tell anyone at all, in case the teacher does anything to Kyle too.
>
> How **appropriate** are each of the following responses by **Kyle** in this situation?
>
> **Question 1:** Reporting the incident to the principal.
>
> (a) A very appropriate thing to do
> (b) Appropriate, but not ideal
> (c) Inappropriate, but not awful
> (d) A very inappropriate thing to do
>
> The correct answer here is B: appropriate, but not ideal. Despite Kyle looking out for his friend, it is important to encourage an individual to report inappropriate behaviour themselves. The most ideal scenario would be for Kyle to explain to Joey why Joey needs to inform the principal of the situation, and then offering to accompany Joey to the principal's office to discuss the serious matter. This takes into consideration the fact that Joey may feel isolated or too scared to tell the principal himself, but still ensures that Joey is the one taking responsibility in reporting the inappropriate actions of his teacher.
>
> Here, it was important that you discerned that the question stem talked about Kyle rather than Joey. If it was Joey, then the answer would have been A ('A very appropriate thing to do') instead of B, since it would've been Joey himself reporting the incident that he was directly involved in.

5.3.5 Short-term and long-term importance

It is important to consider that some responses may be considered important or appropriate in the short-term, as it addresses the problem immediately, while other responses are important or appropriate in the long-term, where it looks at the ripple effects of the problem after the situation, usually long after what is described in the scenario. Usually, the latter is given a higher level of priority, but this depends on the type of situation you are given. Refer below for an example, where the short-term and long-term implications of the issue must be considered.

> **SAMPLE:**
> *Lyra is a barista who has been working at the local café for three months now, ever since she turned 18. It's a very small café, where she works with only her boss and her best friend, Kori, by switching around rosters. One day, Lyra is working alone and a customer, a 70 year old man, comes in with an order she's not particularly familiar with. She puts it into the register and the customer pays in cash. He goes to his table as Lyra discreetly reads the guide on making the specific coffee, following the instructions awkwardly yet finally making a decent cup. She gives the cup to the customer and returns to the register to serve the next customer. However, in the middle of taking the next customer's order, she hears a squeal from the first customer's table and, excusing herself, runs over to check on him. She sees the customer's pants drenched in coffee and he complains to Lyra, saying that the coffee was extremely hot – so hot that his hands violently shook and he instantly dropped it on himself, causing the mess. He demanded a refund and warned that he would sue the café if he didn't get the refund immediately. Lyra was absolutely certain that the coffee wasn't that hot; she tested it a little before pouring it into the customer's cup. She calls her boss and Kori three times each, but neither of them is picking up.*
>
> How **appropriate** are each of the following responses by **Lyra** in this situation?
>
> **Question 1:** Without telling her boss, give the customer their refund.
>
> (a) A very appropriate thing to do
> (b) Appropriate, but not ideal
> (c) Inappropriate, but not awful
> (d) A very inappropriate thing to do
>
> **Question 2:** Tell the customer to stop lying, since it must not have been hot at all, and to get over it.
>
> (a) A very appropriate thing to do
> (b) Appropriate, but not ideal
> (c) Inappropriate, but not awful
> (d) A very inappropriate thing to do
>
> **Question 1: B**
>
> The most ideal scenario would have been for Lyra to notify her boss in some way, whether it be through text message or voice mail, and let him know about the situation. Giving him a refund would be a short-term solution that immediately addresses the upset customer while allowing Lyra to get back to serving others, but does not consider the long-term health implications for the customer if the temperature of the coffee really was that hot. The fact that the customer is elderly must also be considered, since their comparatively frail bodies may not be able to tolerate certain temperatures that Lyra, a young person, would be able to tolerate.
>
> **Question 2: D**
>
> This is a considerably rude and confrontational response and demonstrates a severe lack of professionalism as an employee. Again, it must be considered that people have different tolerances of temperature and pain, and perhaps Lyra was used to a high temperature that a frail elderly person like the 70 year old customer could be severely hurt by. Above all, spilling hot drinks can cause burns of varying severities, and it is likely that the customer's old age could aggravate any burns that have been inflicted on him. It is best for Lyra to instead apologise, help clean up the mess, give the customer his refund and ask him whether she should call emergency services if the burn is causing him great pain.

5.4 Strategy for appropriateness questions

The table below gives a brief definition of each of the options provided to you to choose from.

Option	What it means
"A very appropriate thing to do"	Address at least one feature (does not have to be all features) of the given situation
"Appropriate, but not ideal"	Can be done, but it is not exactly the best or a very good course of action to take
"Inappropriate, but not awful"	It is not ideal at all, and probably should not be done, but it is not totally terrible or a complete disaster if it is pursued
"A very inappropriate thing to do"	Should not be done under any circumstances and will exacerbate (i.e. worsen) the situation

The response that you consider to be correct must be in relation to **what a certain character in the scenario should do,** instead of what they are likely to do based on the circumstances or their character. So, for the specific example about Jessica above, you may interpret the answer options as whether her response makes sense for her as a person and the situation she has been thrown into, in which case you may mistakenly pick option A or B. This is likely to be because of her high level of panic for her friend's condition causing her to not think clearly; hence, Jessica may neglect her duties so her explaining the situation to the patient and leaving immediately is possible, and perhaps likely. But that does not make it appropriately moral, and morality is the true focus of Situational Judgement Test questions, so this should be your primary concern too.

5.5 Strategy for importance questions

The table below gives a brief definition of each of the options provided to you to choose from.

Option	What it means
"Very important"	Crucial course of action to take in relation to the situation
"Important"	Has significance but is not critical to consider
"Of minor importance"	A course of action that could be considered, but it does not really matter if it is pursued or not
"Not important at all"	Definitely should not be considered

This question type may be a bit confusing at first, but it can simply be boiled down to whether a given factor should be considered when making a decision and to what extent. For the first question type, you are given various possible responses for the scenario's issue to judge, but here you are given only one general response (written in the scenario itself) and have to instead **judge various concerns that could affect how someone responds to the situation.** The best way to understand how to answer these questions is to go through a worked example.

SAMPLE :

Thomas is a fourth-year medical student and has made friends with Justin, a third-year medical student who recently started his placement. Thomas and Justin soon add each other on various social media sites. Scrolling through Justin's feed, Thomas quickly notices that every few days, Justin puts up photos of himself at the hospital and sometimes includes sleeping patients, with their names and other personally identifiable information easily visible on the whiteboard next to their beds. This has been going on for a few months in total. Thomas is unsure whether he should raise his concerns about Justin's posts to the appropriate authorities.

How **important** to take into account are the following considerations for **Thomas** when deciding how to respond to the situation?

Question 1: That Justin forgot to blur out the information and faces due to getting burnt out from work.

(a) Very important
(b) Important
(c) Of minor importance
(d) Not important at all

Question 2: The hospital policy specifically stating that photos must not be taken of patients without their consent.

(a) Very important
(b) Important
(c) Of minor importance
(d) Not important at all

Question 1: D

It is irrelevant whether Justin meant to erase the personally identifiable information or not. The issue at hand is whether Thomas tells the suitable authorities about what he's seen or not. He is able to discern private information which should not be made public, which means that Justin has breached patient confidentiality and the appropriate staff must be made aware of this.

Question 2: A

Medical students completing their clinical placements must follow each hospital's policy and regulations, as they have been put in place for many reasons such as the safety of their patients. Taking photos of a patient and releasing them on social media can have many negative consequences, such as the patient being stalked online, or a patient's family, friends, or colleagues finding out about a medical condition the patient wished to keep private.

5.6 Sample questions

SAMPLE :

To celebrate her recent graduation from medical school and to give herself a break before becoming an intern, Joanna is on a cruise to Greece with her high school friends, none of whom studied Medicine. Suddenly, an announcement is made through the PA system asking if a medically qualified person was on board since a medical emergency has occurred. The call is repeated a few times and Joanna's friends are urging her to go, but she remains hesitant as she is not a fully qualified doctor yet. The announcement continues to be repeated and doesn't seem to stop, making her friends and nearby passengers worried. Joanna needs to decide if she should respond to the call or not.

How **important** to take into account are the following considerations for **Joanna** when deciding how to respond to the situation?

Question 1: She is on a holiday now and needs to relax.
  (a) Very important
  (b) Important
  (c) Of minor importance
  (d) Not important at all

Question 2: Even though she graduated, she barely passed her exams.
  (a) Very important
  (b) Important
  (c) Of minor importance
  (d) Not important at all

Question 3: Her friends are now physically pushing her to go and respond to the call.
  (a) Very important
  (b) Important
  (c) Of minor importance
  (d) Not important at all

SAMPLE :

Ashley is a second-year medical student and she has been put into a group with three other second-years, whose names were Zane, Petra, and Bailey, to work on a group project. Unlike the other groups, they all started working seriously on it the week before it was due and only organised one group rehearsal on the morning of their presentation. During this rehearsal, Bailey turned up with a hangover and was very stressed, continually apologising for getting drunk last night. She is still able to talk, remember her lines, and stand in front of the class, but she's worried that she may get the urge to vomit in the middle of the presentation.

How **appropriate** are each of the following responses by **Ashley** in this situation?

Question 4: Comfort Bailey and give her a bottle of water.
  (a) A very appropriate thing to do
  (b) Appropriate, but not ideal
  (c) Inappropriate, but not awful
  (d) A very inappropriate thing to do

Question 5: Divide Bailey's section of the presentation between herself, Zane, and Petra.
  (a) A very appropriate thing to do
  (b) Appropriate, but not ideal
  (c) Inappropriate, but not awful
  (d) A very inappropriate thing to do

5.6 Sample questions

SAMPLE:
Ainsley is a consultant who is working in an Emergency Department. A patient named Carly comes in – she has just started her second semester of first-year Medicine and comes to the department due to a referral from her GP since she has had slightly abnormal ECG results. This morning, she experienced shortness of breath, heart palpitations and other symptoms that closely align with those of a heart attack. However, this is unusual for a young and healthy girl and Ainsley suspects that it may be a panic attack, which can sometimes be detected in an ECG. Ainsley must decide whether she should send Carly home or whether she should investigate further.

Note: An ECG is a medical instrument used to measure the electrical activity of the heart.

How **important** to take into account are the following considerations for **Ainsley** when deciding how to respond to the situation?

Question 6: A blood test conducted by the GP, to further verify whether it is a heart issue, returns abnormal results.
- (a) Very important
- (b) Important
- (c) Of minor importance
- (d) Not important at all

Question 7: The ECG results may have an error.
- (a) Very important
- (b) Important
- (c) Of minor importance
- (d) Not important at all

Question 8: Ainsley has recently developed anxiety issues.
- (a) Very important
- (b) Important
- (c) Of minor importance
- (d) Not important at all

SAMPLE:
Two first-year medical students, Lachlan and Sam, have their final clinical assessment of the year before their end-of-semester exams. To pass their first year, students must participate in all of their assessments and receive an overall pass mark. Sam has voiced her concern to Lachlan about their upcoming assessment, which involves a physical examination of the heart on a simulated patient. Sam tells Lachlan she has not studied for this assessment, and her grades this entire year have been average at best. Now, minutes before they enter the medical building to do their assessment, Sam is in tears, has trouble breathing, and tells Lachlan that she feels like fainting and wants to go home.

How **appropriate** are each of the following responses by **Lachlan** in this situation?

Question 9: Try and make Sam relax and make her do breathing and mindfulness exercises.
- (a) A very appropriate thing to do
- (b) Appropriate, but not ideal
- (c) Inappropriate, but not awful
- (d) A very inappropriate thing to do

Question 10: Tell Sam that she needs to participate in this final assessment to at least have a chance at passing.
- (a) A very appropriate thing to do
- (b) Appropriate, but not ideal
- (c) Inappropriate, but not awful
- (d) A very inappropriate thing to do

5.7 Answers to sample questions

Question 1: D
The matter has been declared a medical emergency, so it means that the problem needs to be dealt with urgently and there's a need for someone with at least some advanced training. Therefore, Joanna needs to put aside the fact that she is on a holiday and respond as soon as possible, otherwise someone's life could potentially be at risk.

Question 2: C
Despite Joanna not being fully qualified yet, she will soon become an intern and work as a junior doctor at hospitals, so she is highly likely to be able to effectively handle a medical emergency. A doctor's grades in medical school is a relatively unimportant factor, as it does not attest to their capability in a practical situation; sometimes the best doctors were not the best academically. So the assumption that she cannot help just because she barely passed should not be made; a doctor who passes medical school is a doctor who can assist society, regardless of their exact numerical results on assessment tasks.

Question 3: C
Joanna needs to remain calm in this situation and take the appropriate course of action in spite of how panicked her friends might be. However, this is a minor factor to consider as Joanna is in a position to calm her friends down by responding to the situation accordingly

Question 4: A
Helping Bailey calm down is an entirely appropriate action to take, particularly as a fellow team member. Reducing her stress and giving her water can help with her hangover, and ultimately may make her capable of presenting with the rest of the team.

Question 5: C
While this may allow Bailey to have a rest and let her hangover pass, it is unfair on the rest of the team members, including Ashley. This may also offend Bailey since she is still able to present. The best scenario would be the team rehearsing amongst themselves as best they could and seeing how Bailey goes. Before the presentation, the person who will be marking the presentation should be notified of Bailey's condition. However, if Bailey's condition gets any worse towards the end or during the presentation, then the team can request an opportunity to present together at a later date.

Question 6: A
Having abnormal levels of compounds in her blood that are directly associated with heart issues is vital information that needs to be considered when making Carly's diagnosis.

Question 7: C
While this may be a minor factor to keep in factor, there must still be a reason behind her worrying symptoms, so further investigation is still required, and another ECG can easily be done.

Question 8: B
This is a relatively important factor to keep in mind since it supports the possible diagnosis that Carly had a panic attack. However, having a history of anxiety does not rule out the fact that she may have other heart issues. So while the possibility that she had a panic attack is increased, due to her history of anxiety, this does not completely rule out the possibility that she has underlying heart issues as well.

Question 9: A
Calming Sam down is a wholly appropriate action to take, as she needs to be relaxed and minimise her anxiety. This will assist her with going into the assessment with a clearer mind, which will help with meeting the criteria to gain higher marks.

Question 10: C
Though this statement may be factually correct, telling Sam something that she already knows is unlikely to help with reducing her anxiety, and may in fact worsen it. This is not a completely terrible response, as Lachlan is essentially just explaining the reality of Sam's situation to her, but it is ultimately inappropriate as it is unlikely to make Sam feel any better.

Section 6
UCAT preparation advice

6.1 Practice questions

Whilst many may argue that the UCAT is not something that you can prepare for, this statement has been refuted multiple times by those who have achieved a high score. In saying this, it is important to keep in mind exactly what kind of preparation you are doing, since you will need to make the most of the time you have until the exam. Your first priority should be familiarising yourself with what the exam consists of and gathering as much knowledge as you can about its **format,** its **sections,** and the **types of questions** that come up – which is what this book aims to help you with! Your next priority is to keep practising questions for all five sections until you can recognise patterns in both the question types and the answers.

To prepare for the UCAT in general, the first step you should take is to complete the **free official questions and practice papers offered by the UCAT Consortium** on their website. This is the official organisation that writes the UCAT, and they offer:

- A question tutorial, which gives advice for each of the five sub-tests
- A tour tutorial, which explains the format of the real exam and its many functions, such as how to activate the on-screen calculator and how to flag a question for review
- 3 timed full practice exams
- A question bank consisting of 400+ questions!

Working through all of these resources will give you the best indication about the style and most probable difficulty of questions that will appear in the real test. In addition, you can try the **1000+ free practice questions on the official UCAT website,** which are equally high-quality. You may also find older resources for the UKCAT (the previous name of this test) which will still be relevant for the current UCAT.

Next, make the best use of all the free resources for the UCAT that you can find online. There are a copious amount of YouTube videos made by previous UKCAT/UCAT candidates who scored highly, giving their own personal experiences with the exam and tips on how to do well overall or in specific sections. Free UCAT guides are also available to read online, but the best one would be the official guide written by the UCAT Consortium.

Then, if you really want to, you can consider purchasing a UCAT package from a preparation company. The UCAT Consortium does not have any association with these companies, hence do not advocate for how reliable their material is and rather warn against using their resources, especially since they are often highly expensive. Additionally, doing company preparation does not guarantee a high score, particularly since their practice exams sometimes include marking schemes which can be misleading and not portray how the results are actually calculated, providing an inaccurate indication of your progress.

6.2 Exam strategies

The most important part about UCAT preparation is taking it seriously, as it is an exam you can **learn how to tackle.** Make a **flexible schedule** that allocates regular UCAT practice in between studying for your school assessment tasks, extracurricular activities, and any other responsibilities. While some say that you should give yourself at least one or two months before your booked date to prepare, the most appropriate amount and period of time for preparation depends on each person and their capabilities. However, you should start as soon as you can, in case you end up requiring extra time to understand a certain concept – you don't want to leave anything to the last minute!

When you sit your first few practice exams and you find that you are not doing as well as you want, don't worry! Focus on the questions you got wrong and re-evaluate your thought process which led to the incorrect answer. Keep a record of the questions you got wrong for each of the sections in a separate document, so that you can look back and notice a pattern in your working that needs to be changed. If this list is getting too long, pick the main questions which come under a specific type (e.g. for Abstract Reasoning, if you keep struggling with 'Next in the Sequence', pick the select few questions where you had the greatest difficulty finding any sort of pattern). **Track your progress** for your practice exams, perhaps by making a table which incorporates when you sat the exam, the raw marks for each section, the overall raw mark, and any notes to yourself on where you went wrong, how to improve, and what to do in the following practice test.

If you find yourself skipping a few days of practice, or losing motivation for UCAT study, that's okay too. Just try changing your schedule around a bit and search for the root of your decreasing motivation. For example, are you doing the same kind of question for a particular section over and over again, perhaps because it is your weakest section? While it is important to address your weaknesses, **don't neglect your stronger areas;** in fact, you should aim to master a few sections and question types as this can eventually give your overall aggregate a massive boost. Practice a variety of questions from each of the sub-tests, but do more from the section you are most confident in when you feel a bit demotivated.

Finally, since time is such a crucial factor in the exam, practice in **fully timed conditions** with most, if not all, of your practice exams. In addition, ensure you complete all of these practice tests in exam conditions (e.g. use the on-screen calculator, instead of a real calculator when doing a Quantitative Reasoning question or practice test).

6.3 Advice for sitting the UCAT

Firstly, make sure you arrange your booking and related fees early so you are **registered before the deadline.** By doing this early, there is a greater likelihood that you can book your preferred date and time, and you can reschedule if needed, whereas leaving this until the last minute won't give you as much flexibility. While this is a simple first step, there are plenty of stories of UCAT candidates being so caught up in their test preparation that they forget to register in time and were unable to sit the exam, so just get your booking done as soon as possible!

Additionally, **book your exam date for early July** if possible. This is the best time to get the test over and done with before your summer break. This way, you can focus on sitting your UCAT exam without the extra stress for your A-Levels studies, and once it's over, you can put the UCAT behind you and get back to focusing on your subjects. To further support this, the UCAT Consortium conducted interviews and research with previous candidates and found that those who took the exam early usually ended up with a result they were more satisfied with!

It is highly recommended that you reschedule your booked date if you are feeling unwell, physically or mentally, in spite of the fact that you may lose your test fee. If you arrive at the exam at your initial date, your presence declares that you are fit, so you can't decide halfway through the exam that you aren't feeling well and want to try again another day! However, if you cannot complete the test at all due to illness, you must inform your exam invigilator/supervisor, then directly email the UCAT Office, with supporting documents for medical evidence in order for your test to be rescheduled. This is another good reason for arranging your test date in early July – if your booked date is in the last weeks of September, the UCAT Office may not be able to reschedule your test and, consequently, you may have to sit the test in the following year.

On the test day, you need to arrive at least 15 minutes before the time you booked so that you can check-in. At the reception desk, you must present a printout of the Pearson VUE confirmation email and one appropriate piece of **photo identification** (such as a passport or learner's driving license). Ensure that the name and date of birth displayed on your photo ID matches the details given upon registration. Also, note that a student/employer ID card or a library card are NOT appropriate forms of photo ID.

Before the exam commences, ensure that you have access to a working pen and laminated booklet, or request these if you do not. Moreover, if you experience illness, problems with software/hardware, or any other disturbances, you need to immediately notify your invigilator.

When sitting the exam, try to employ the **keyboard shortcuts** to make the most efficient use of your limited testing time. The shortcuts available are listed below.

- **Alt + P** = Previous question
- **Alt + N** = Next question
- **Alt + F** = Flag the current question for review
- **Alt + C** = Activate the calculator

However, in order to select an option for a question, you must either use your mouse to click on the option or drag and drop the answer. If you want to use the calculator with your keyboard, ensure that 'Num Lock' is on so that the number pad works. To close the calculator, you can simply close it, click away, or move on to another question.

You are also allowed to write on their piece of laminated paper during instruction reading time. Whilst you cannot read the actual questions, your spare time after reading and understanding the instructions can be well spent by physically noting down helpful hints. This is most relevant for the Abstract Reasoning section, where it is recommended by high scorers that you jot down your bank of potential patterns so that you can refer to them during that sub-test.

For each sub-test, all the questions are worth the same mark, despite the different levels of difficulty, and incorrect questions will not lead to marks being deducted. Therefore, it is best to **make educated guesses and flag the harder questions for review** so you can come back to them at the end if possible. In case you do not end up with enough time to review them, you will at the very least have an educated guess for all questions, and thus you are more likely to get a higher mark than if you simply skip anything tricky and run out of time, or if you were to waste too much time on the harder questions and lose marks on the easier ones.

Ultimately, no matter what you do, you will be pressed for time, so keep track of how long you have left using the **timer** on the top right corner of the screen. However, don't look at it too often, as this can become a cause of unnecessary stress and will inevitably lead you to wasting precious time. This is particularly important if you have been noticing that a certain question is taking you a while to figure out, in which case you should guess, flag for review, and then move on.

Most importantly though, **relax and stay calm** throughout the exam. It's a huge advantage to have a clear head and to be able to pay careful attention to key words, thus decreasing the chance of making silly mistakes. There will be other candidates around you in the test centre, so do not panic if you see or hear some people clicking away to the next question at a much faster rate than you, or leaving the exam early. Focus on the current question and just block out your surroundings to give yourself the best chance at success!

Part II

Medical interviews

Section 1
Interview advice

Before we get into the advice, if you have attained an interview offer from any university offering an undergraduate medical course, then congratulations! You are now one step closer to achieving a place in Medicine. Many would argue that the interview is the hardest component of medical entrance and, unfortunately, the criterion that is often underestimated. Just like with the UCAT and your A-Levels studies, preparation and lots of practice is key to performing well and impressing your interviewers. For Medicine, the most common forms of the interview are the **semi-structural/semi-structured/panel (SS) interview** or the **multiple mini interview (MMI).**

In a semi-structural interview, you usually have to face a panel of two or three interviewers who ask you a variety of questions. These will range from **general questions** such as "Why do you want to become a doctor?" to questions that concern a given **scenario,** such as "if you were this person, what do you think would be the best course of action and why?" Each university that has a semi-structural interview will have a different structure.

The multiple mini interview tends to have **8 active stations** (in total there are 9, with one being a 'rest' station) for domestic students, and 4 active stations for international students (or 5 in total, with one 'rest' station). Each station goes for **10 minutes** total, with 2 minutes reading time and 8 minutes of answering time, with one interviewer per station. Once these 10 minutes are over, you are told to move on to the next question and repeat the process, with a different interviewer and a different scenario. The kind of questions that can appear in a station can vary significantly.

Below is a table that covers whether a university offers an interview and which type of interview is offered for different universities, though you should always consult with the university websites as this information can change each year.

1.1 SS panel universities and dates

SS panel interviews					
University	**Approx interview dates**				
	Nov	**Dec**	**Jan**	**Feb**	**Mar**
Barts (Queen Mary)			■	■	
Cambridge University		■			
Glasgow University	■	■	■	■	■
Oxford University		■			
Swansea University				■	■

1.2 MMI universities and dates

MMI interviews							
University	**Approx interview dates**						
	Nov	Dec	Jan	Feb	Mar	Apr	May
Aberdeen University		■	■	■	■	■	
Anglia Ruskin University		■	■				
Aston University		■	■		■		
Birmingham University			■	■			
Brighton and Sussex Medical School			■	■			
Bristol University		■	■	■			
Buckingham University			■		■	■	■
Brunel University			■	■	■	■	■
Cardiff University		■		■			
University of Central Lancashire		■	■	■	■		■
University College London		■	■	■	■		
Dundee University		■	■	■			
Edge Hill University		■			■		
Edinburgh University		■	■		■		
Exeter University		■	■	■	■		
Hull York Medical School		■	■	■			
Imperial College London			■	■			
Keele University		■	■	■	■		
Kent and Medway Medical School			■	■	■		
King's College London	■	■	■	■	■	■	■
Lancaster University			■				
Leeds University		■	■				
Leicester University		■	■				
Liverpool University		■	■	■			
Newcastle University		■	■	■			
Norwich (UEA) Medical School	■	■	■	■	■	■	

University	Approx interview dates						
	Nov	Dec	Jan	Feb	Mar	Apr	May
Nottingham University		■	■	■	■		
Plymouth University			■	■			
Queen's University Belfast		■	■	■			
Sheffield University		■	■		■		
Southampton University			■	■	■		
St Andrews University	■	■	■	■	■		
St George's University	■	■		■	■		
Sunderland University		■	■				
Warwick University		■	■				

If you have been offered an interview from a university that is far away from where you live, you must make the appropriate **travel arrangements** to be able to attend your interview for the booked time and date. Whilst this information may seem obvious, universities often get questions from students who expect these arrangements to be arranged for them, so make sure you get on top of this yourself! If you are not able to make it to your interview, and can no longer reschedule it, the university cannot consider you for a medical place. If you decline or cancel your interview, the interview place will be given to the candidate next in line, who otherwise would have missed out.

Many universities have stipulated that **applicants can only attend their interview once,** regardless of the number of times they apply for the program. In other words, if you have graduated from sixth form in 2024, attained an interview offer for 2025 entry, sat the interview, did not gain a place and decided to take a gap year to re-apply in 2025 for 2026 entry, you will not receive an interview offer again. Your place will be determined by your A-Levels results you achieved in 2024, your UCAT score (which you will have to sit in 2025), and your previous interview performance in 2024. This highlights the importance of performing to the highest standard you can in the interview for the first time around, since that will be your only chance at that particular institution.

In terms of what to wear to your interviews, **semi-formal dress** is usually preferred by the universities, so you should aim for a conservative and neat look. Ensure that what you wear is comfortable as well, since you will be in that attire for a long time in total, considering the actual interview and the typically long waiting time before it! As a general guideline, for boys, a collared business shirt and trousers (dress pants) are enough (tie is optional) and for girls, a collared shirt or blouse and a business skirt (not any shorter than just a little above the knee) or trousers are sufficient. If it is really cold on the day of your interview, you can wear a heavier coat, scarf, and gloves for the journey and just take them off once you're inside. There is no restriction for wearing attire for religious reasons, such as a kippah, turban, or headscarf along with a long skirt. You should not come to the interview in revealing clothing and anything that is flashy and may create a bad first impression. On the other hand, avoid wearing a suit or anything extremely formal for your medical interview as this will make you seem over-dressed. In fact, some universities specifically state that a suit should *not* be worn. Nevertheless, your outfit is not a strict component of the interviewers' criteria, so you shouldn't worry about it too much as long as it is not completely casual or messy.

1.3 Why choose Medicine

Disclaimer: *As we both had to sign confidentiality agreements, we cannot disclose which questions we were asked in our own interviews for any of the universities we applied to. The common general questions that are listed here are just that: common. We cannot guarantee that you will get asked any of these in the real interview, although there is a very high likelihood that you may. These should be taken as indicative questions that give you an idea of what to expect, and not a comprehensive list of questions for any particular university.*

Interviews are a fantastic way to demonstrate how motivated you are to study to become a medical practitioner. Since the interview is so focused on assessing your **personal traits** and who you are as a person, one of the best ways to cultivate natural answers is through **self-reflection.** Think to yourself about why exactly you have gone through all the effort of studying for the UCAT and filling out all the numerous forms and applications for each university, and finally studying for the interview. Ask yourself why exactly you want to study Medicine. Be honest with yourself and write down a list of all the reasons, big and small. Consider:

- Have you had any personal or volunteering experiences with the healthcare system?
- Since when have you wanted to apply for Medicine, and what sparked this decision?
- Do you personally know or have you spoken with any medical practitioners about their experiences?
- Is there a particular vision you have of yourself working in a specific field?
- What traits do you possess that would make you a valuable addition to the medical system?
- What is it about Medicine that you find fascinating, exciting, or rewarding?
- Why does Medicine appeal to you more than other potential career paths?

After you have written down all your reasons, play the devil's advocate and **critically evaluate each reason.** For instance, if one of your reasons for applying is because you like helping people, what about other healthcare courses such as nursing, physiotherapy, or counselling, all of which have a strong core of helping individuals and communities?

The reason for this little exercise, and probably the most important consideration for these questions, is to ensure that you are **entering Medicine for the 'right' reasons.** In other words, you should not be applying for and entering Medicine solely due to factors like the high salary that the profession is associated with, the job security or status and prestige behind becoming a doctor, or because of pressures and expectations of your family and peers. It is alright if these are secondary or minor concerns that have influenced your decision, but it is very important that you have at least some sort of genuine interest in the field itself. Medicine, whilst extremely rewarding, is an incredibly hard course, and having no interest in it will make the intensive workload, content, hours, and handling other commitments on the side exponentially difficult.

However, if you don't immediately have a 'good' answer to this question, the best thing to do is to **broaden your perspective.** Maybe you only initially applied because your parents told you to, and because you know becoming a doctor is associated with success and prestige. But if you're seriously considering this career path, do some more research and talk to people with valuable insights. If you have done any medical work experience of volunteering, talk to the practitioners you've worked with to get a sense of their priorities, commitments, and outlook on studying Medicine. Even talking to your local GP, or a friend or relative who is a doctor can be incredibly valuable. Ask them why they chose to enter Medicine – what was their personal journey, what are some positives and negatives of the career, and what do they think are common misconceptions about being a doctor? Talk to more than one person, if possible, to gain an even broader perspective based on a variety of people's experiences, and talk to current or recently graduated medical students to increase your knowledge about the course itself and what you may be getting yourself into. Overall, developing a **realistic, instead of an idealistic, perception of Medicine** is imperative to either finding a real fascination for the field or considering another pathway. After appraising your motivation for trying to get into Medicine, you can get started with some more in-depth preparation.

1.4 Interview preparation

Just like the UCAT, the interview is undoubtedly a test that you can prepare for. Many tend to falsely assume that the interview is just a matter of simply talking to the interviewers, so they do not practise as much as they should, and end up not doing as well as they could have. In the actual interview, this may result in answers which are superficial or one-sided, showcasing a lack of adequate thought, preparation, or depth. On the other side of the spectrum, other candidates may take the interview too seriously and end up 'over-practising.' Thus, they become stressed and exhausted, and their answers often come out rehearsed and insincere rather than natural, honest responses. These same people may also make the mistake of memorising answers to common questions from past medical students or other resources, particularly if these answers do not align with their own beliefs yet sound impressive and sophisticated. With their prior training, the interviewers are often very good at detecting answers that are disingenuous, so anyone attempting to rote learn responses is highly unlikely to gain as many marks as someone who prepares adequately and answers thoughtfully. Considering this, your approach to interview preparation should be **balanced** and geared towards explaining your **genuine beliefs and values** in an **articulate, professional, and confident manner.**

You should start the process of preparation before you get the interview offer, especially if you feel that you have a good chance of getting one with your predicted grades and UCAT scores. Even if you do not get an interview offer, it remains as good practice for the future if you are planning on applying for Medicine in later years or as a postgraduate course. The reason why you should start early is that the period of time between the interview offer and the timeframe for booking your interview is often quite short (especially if you are an IB applicant).

The specifics of how you should prepare depends on the type of medical interview you are sitting. You should start by answering some of the most common general questions for a semi-structural interview, or a few easy scenarios and related questions for an MMI. Get as much practice as you can and make this practice regular, gradually increasing the frequency as you get closer to your interview date. However, ensure you don't overwork yourself and burn out by occasionally taking a break from preparation, since it may decrease your overall motivation to continue practising in the long-term.

Practise by yourself first, and then **in front of a mirror** (even if it feels awkward at first!) – this enables you to take note of your body language and facial expressions, increasing your awareness of how you may look in front of the interviewer and allowing you to make any preliminary adjustments. If it helps, you can draw a smiley face on a sticky note and stick that onto the mirror, so that you have a figure to focus on as you speak! From here, you can start practising in front of your family and friends, and encourage them to give feedback on your content and delivery. However, be mindful that your parents and peers may not provide as much constructive criticism, and that the answers they perceive as good may not be seen in the same light by your interviewers.

So, beyond this, try to **practise with other candidates, or (even better) current medical students.** Connecting with people who have been through this process, even if you can only do so online/virtually, is always valuable. Due to their increased knowledge of the interview process, their feedback will likely be far more specific and useful to you. Some students are afraid that practising with other candidates, who they may view as their 'competition,' may mean that their own 'good' answers will be stolen. However, the reality is that there is so much mutual benefit to practising and critiquing one another that if anything, you are just increasing the likelihood that you will both be admitted into the course! Furthermore, as mentioned previously, rote learning someone else's answer is no guarantee for success – the interviewers are trained to distinguish genuine responses from pre-learned, dishonest pandering.

The best-case scenario, however, would be to have your answers evaluated by someone with past experience as an interviewer, but you need to be careful that this person is not a member of the panel for the year of your application. In fact, usually before your interview, you will be asked by staff members to confirm and declare that you have no association with any of the interviewers and, if you later find out that you do, you must report it to them immediately.

In terms of what to practice, you should **first work on what you want to say before improving how you say it.** For an open-ended question, aim to give around 2 or 3 points and back each of them up with explanations if you can. For example, for the question "Why do you want to become a doctor?" the three points you may want to come up with can come under three categories: work experience, personal experience, and the fascinating aspects of the course itself which sets it apart from other courses. Perhaps you were in the hospital for some time as a child, and the care of your doctor inspired you to consider the career. This interest grew when you exposed yourself to what the job involves via work experience program in a hospital. Finally, you can detail the specific features of the course itself that you find interesting, such as the opportunities for further study that foster life-long learning, and strong integration of problem-solving and real-world applications in assessment tasks.

There are all sorts of 'Frequently Asked Questions' and online lists of questions that are likely to come up in medical interviews, so collate as many as you can so that you have a good frame of reference for your practice. Below are some examples of the general questions only, since scenario-type questions vary greatly each year and between different universities.

1.5 List of potential interview questions

Personal questions

- Introduce yourself. / Describe yourself. / Tell us about yourself.
- How do you think a stranger would describe you? / How would your peers describe you?
- What is your greatest strength?
- What is your greatest weakness?
- What are your hobbies? / What do you do in your free time?
- What responsibilities do you have? / Are you a responsible person?
- How would you describe your time management skills?
- What are your priorities in life? / What goals do you have for the future?
- Tell us about your biggest achievement.
- Tell us about the most difficult time in your life. How did you get through it?
- What would you change about yourself if you could?
- Have you ever dealt with failure? If so, how did you overcome it?
- How do you know when you need to seek help?
- What does empathy mean to you?
- How do you learn best?

Studying Medicine questions

- Why do you want to become a doctor? / Why do you want to study Medicine? Why not another health course, such as nursing or physiotherapy?
- If you did not gain a place in Medicine, what would be your next steps?
- What do you expect will be challenging about studying Medicine?
- What do you know about our medical course?
- Why do you deserve a place studying Medicine over other candidates?
- Why do you want to study at this specific university? / What do you know about studying Medicine at this specific university?
- What would you do if you received a poor grade in one of your subjects at university?
- What would you do if you felt overwhelmed during your studies?

Life as a doctor questions

- Why do you think you would make a good doctor?
- What are the traits of a good doctor?
- What are some good aspects of being a doctor? / What aspects of being a doctor appeal to you?
- What are the drawbacks of being a doctor? / What aspects of being a doctor do not appeal to you?

Work experiences and teamwork

- Did you do any sort of work experience in a health setting? If so, tell us about it. / Tell us about any work experience you have done.
- Tell us about a time when you worked in a team. Was there any conflict? If so, how did you deal with it? Do you think there could have been a better way to deal with it?
- In a team setting, are you usually the leader or a team member? Do you think one is better than the other? If so, why?
- What are the traits of a good team leader and why?
- What are the traits of a good team member and why?
- Tell us about what you would do if one of your team members weren't co-operating or doing their share of the workload.
- Tell me about a time when you have encountered a communication breakdown. Did you learn anything from this? In the future and in a similar situation, would you change your approach or deal with it in a different way, and how?
- Tell us about a time when you were stressed. How did you deal with the stress? Is this how you usually deal with stress?
- Tell us about a time when you had to work with negative feedback. How did you receive it?

Interest in the medical field

- Is there an area you would like to specialise in? If so, why? / What kind of speciality do you want to do? Why?
- Is there an area you would not like to specialise in? If so, why? / What kind of speciality would you not prefer to do? Why?
- Have you read any medical publications? / Tell us about a medical issue you have read about.
- What is your opinion about the state of the medical profession currently?
- What do you think is the most exciting recent medical development?
- What do you think is the biggest challenge that medical professionals have to face today?
- What do you think the field of medicine will look like in the future?

Ethical issues

- Euthanasia
- Abortion
- LGBTQIA+ rights
- Suicide
- Bullying
- Postcode lottery
- Anti-vaxxers/vaccination
- Alt-right movement
- NHS funding

- Global warming
- Gender pay gap
- Rights of smokers
- Winter Fuel Payment
- Privacy (especially online)
- Legalisation of marijuana
- Immigration
- Overpopulation
- Doctor strikes

- Capital punishment
- Pharmaceutical industry
- Freedom of speech
- Domestic violence
- Stem cell research
- Designer babies
- Gun laws
- Censorship
- Offshore detention centres

1.5 List of potential interview questions

This is not an exhaustive list, especially since the range of questions that a university will ask depends on what they are specifically looking for in their candidates. Your interviewers may also ask you some extremely **personal questions,** such as "What was your childhood like?" and "Describe your parents. What are they like? How close are you with them?" but these are not too common. Some universities may also base their interview questions around the specific answers you have given in your application. For instance, if one of the application questions asked you to describe some experiences you would like to have in 10 years, and you listed your desire to be involved in curing life-threatening diseases, your interviewers may then ask you about your reasons for this particular desire. This would then be a good opportunity to expand upon your answer if there was a restrictive word count in the original application.

It is important to give answers which cover a **variety of perspectives** so that you don't seem superficial or narrow-minded. For instance, suppose you are given a scenario where a person is conflicted between work and family commitments and you are asked what you would do. Rather than only saying that you would go to work, if this was your choice, consider mentioning that you would explain to your family why you need to prioritse your work in order to help them see things from your point of view, whilst also assuring them that they are just as important to you. On the other hand, if you wanted to do the opposite, consider discussing how you would try to negotiate with your boss to see if you could take some days off to fulfil these family commitments.

This process does require some creativity, and in the real interview some quick thinking too, so a major proportion of your preparation should be allocated to quickly working through these kinds of scenarios. Instead of passively looking at a question and thinking of all the different points to your answer in your head, try to **type or write it all down,** or just answer verbally and **record yourself** using your phone. Try doing this in **timed conditions**, giving yourself **one minute** to answer a question, then afterwards see if you could have expanded upon anything if given more time. Also, try to become detailed but concise in your answers by editing your responses to remove any waffling or repetition so that you get to the point quickly. This will not only help you gain marks more efficiently, but also helps to make a positive impression on the assessor as you will be showcasing clear and effective communication skills in order to respond to their questions and hold their attention. This particularly applies to MMI practice, where time is of the essence and you will be more likely to finish a station on time or with extra time left, thus allowing you to improve any answer you had already given.

Next, employ strategies to improve the **delivery** of what you say. In most cases, what seems to happen that is that a candidate has their developed answer in their head, but they cannot convey it eloquently and its insightfulness almost falls apart. Even if you think of yourself as a social and articulate person, in an interview setting you may become really nervous, possibly because you are not as comfortable as you tend to be with your friends and colleagues. This is completely normal and can be overcome with the right method and amount of practice. Start with just saying what is in your head out loud and with confidence, whether it be to yourself or with another person. Note the tone and volume in which you spoke, non-verbal cues, how many times you may have been tongue-tied, and the confidence with which you translated the abstract thought into verbal speech. Were you too quiet or too loud? Did you sound monotonous? Were you expressionless? Did the answer sound better in your head? Now that you said it aloud, could it be perceived as biased, offensive, or short-sighted? Having another person to listen to what you say can help add some valuable perspective and possibly objectivity to your current performance and what you need to work on. It is alright if you aren't totally happy with your reflection on the first go, because what matters is the feedback you receive and whether you try to improve from then on!

In the practice sessions after this, take on board the feedback from the session before and build upon your delivery bit by bit. Don't expect to suddenly become the best interviewee you can be after one or two practice rounds. This further reinforces the importance of leaving yourself plenty of time for preparation, whether it means a few weeks or a month, depending on your level of confidence. If it helps, you can track your level of progress and the kind of feedback you have gotten each time, ensuring you include what you did well and any new areas of improvement for next time.

1.5 List of potential interview questions

Below is an excerpt of one of many ways in which you can do this.

	Interview type	Uni	What I did	Reflection/feedback
1	SS	Cambridge	Practised common general questions: – Why do you want to be a doctor? – Why do you want to study at Cambridge? – What does it take to be a good doctor?	– Good use of personal experience – Slightly superficial answers – Forgot to mention interest in research for "why Cambridge?" – Was a little quiet/mumbled – Fiddled a lot, which was distracting – Slouched
2	SS	Cambridge	Practised a scenario and three more common general questions: – What are some good aspects of being a doctor? – What are some bad aspects of being a doctor? – Did you do any kind of work experience in the health field? – What do you know about rural and Indigenous health concerns? Also practised 'Why do you want to be a doctor?' and 'Why do you want to study at Cambridge?' again	– Good empathy towards characters in the scenario – A bit monotonous and expressionless – Could have been more balanced in my scenario answers – Listed more good than bad aspects, which could insinuate that I don't have a realistic view of Medicine – My answer to "why do you want to be a doctor?" slightly better, in terms of delivery and covering a few more points (felt more insightful) – Couldn't answer questions about euthanasia. Need to do more research here!
3	SS	Oxford	Practised a scenario and two common general questions: – Why do you want to study at Oxford? – Tell me about a time you worked in a team and whether there was any conflict.	– Took less time to read the scenario – Should have two more points about why Oxford in addition to liking their tutorial system – Couldn't properly explain the team situation
4	SS	Oxford	Practised two scenarios, in timed conditions (gave myself around 30 minutes in total)	– Could articulate two issues and a way to improve each issue slightly better – Almost ran out of time to answer the last question for the second scenario

1.5 List of potential interview questions

5	SS	Oxford	Practised two scenarios, in timed conditions, and three common general questions: – Tell me about a time when you were stressed. How did you deal with the stress? Is this how you usually deal with stress? – Tell me about a time when you had to work with negative feedback. How did you receive it? – Have you ever dealt with failure? If so, how did you overcome it?	– Took less time to read and understand the scenario – Waffled about the stress scenario. Felt that maybe it wasn't all that relevant, but at the last minute thought of a much better example of a memory I should talk about next time. Maybe include some strategies that I know other people use, such as meditation, as a way of showing the interviewer that I could try these as well (shows self-reflection) – Remembered to smile! :) – Tried to be a little more passionate in my tone; 'interviewer' said it was better than being monotonous like before
6	MMI	Imperial College London	Practised one scenario, with five questions, in timed conditions (because it's stricter with time, so I might as well start practising in timed conditions from the start). Gave myself 10 minutes total, 2 minutes reading time and 8 minutes speaking time, just like the real thing	– Had to read the question two times after reading time to fully understand it – Ran out of time for the last question – Answers were superficial, could've said one or two more points for each, even if it was brief – Said a lot of "um"s and "ah"s – Felt rushed for time – A lot of waffling and couldn't get my points across for most of the questions
7	SS	Cambridge	Practised two scenarios and one ethical question (abortion)	– Managed to be a bit more balanced for the first scenario – Completely screwed up the second scenario; had a mental blank and let stress get the better of me :(– Gave three points each for and against abortion but need to be clearer with what my own opinion is; seemed a bit too wishy-washy

1.5 List of potential interview questions

8	MMI	Imperial College London	Practised one scenario with five questions, in timed conditions	– Remembered to enter the room confidently, smile, and introduce myself – Got onto the last question but ran out of time to finish my answer – Scored 3/4 for one question, but only scored 1 or 2 for the others – Had to ask the 'interviewer' to repeat questions twice – Felt a little less stressed and recovered well
9	MMI	Imperial College London	Practised two scenarios with five questions each, in timed conditions	– Managed to barely finish all the questions on time for the first scenario – Surprisingly finished early for the second scenario – Answers to the first scenario were average (got 2/4 for all except one 3/4) – Answers to the second scenario were pretty good (got 3/4 for three and 2/4 for the rest) due to thoughtful answers – Waffled a bit less
10	SS	Oxford	Practised two scenarios, one ethical question (No Jab, No Pay) and two common general questions in timed conditions: – Is there an area you would like to specialise in? Why? – Tell me about a time when there was a communication breakdown. Did you learn anything from this? In the future and in a similar situation, would you change your approach or deal with it in a different way, and how?	– Understood both scenarios pretty well and quickly – Answers were mostly thoughtful; just screwed up a couple of questions for the second scenario – For the ethical question, stated my own opinion first and then went on to explain both sides of the argument. Had three arguments for either side, but the 'don't agree' side's arguments were a little superficial - Had no idea about the specialisations. Should research this. - Thought of a really good teamwork conflict situation I had recently in my school club. Could explain this in a detailed and engaging way. Should suggest one more way which I could've changed my approach

This table is just a made up example, hence why some of the feedback is quite vague. When you do this yourself, you can add as much detail as you want, including the date of each session, how long each session went for, and more **specific remarks for improvement.** For example, if you received feedback for practising the ethical segment for an SS panel interview, briefly state the points that you made in the session, which of these points you could have taken out or improve upon, and which other points you should have added to improve your answer. Similarly, for the scenarios, you may also want to make a brief summary of what it entailed and what the most important parts were.

Once you have more confidence in the quality of your answers, a lot of practice with saying these answers out loud, and are more comfortable in the interview setting in general, it will become so much easier to treat the interview as a **conversation** and **be friendly** to your interviewers. In doing so, as stated in countless job interview advice articles, your stress levels decrease immensely and your answers start to naturally flow. This lets you minimise the negative **distress** that causes mental blanks and can make you stumble, exacerbating your nervousness, and leaves you with only the positive kind of stress – **eustress** – that improves your alertness, concentration, and

If you have attained more than one interview offer, and are planning to attend more than one interview, it would also be a good idea to keep track of how your previous interviews went. Designing a table that is similar to the one above, you can keep track of what type of interview it was, which university it was at, what happened before and during the interview, what questions were asked, and how you think you went. Use this as feedback to use for your next attempt, especially if it is the same type of interview.

Also, remember that although the university and your interviewers will not expect you to have an in-depth knowledge of specific medical issues and medical terminology, it is important to be familiar with a few essential components of **medical ethics.** These are:

- Privacy and confidentiality
- The no-harm principle
- Patient autonomy
- Informed consent

Privacy relates to restricted public access of information in the healthcare field, and **confidentiality** relates to the medical professional's respect for their patient's privacy. The **no-harm principle** is fairly self-explanatory – it just means that a healthcare professional should never intentionally injure their patient in any way, physically or mentally. **Patient autonomy** refers to the fact that patients are self-governing and can make their own health decisions when deemed competent. Finally, before any history taking or medical procedure, a patient must give their **informed consent,** where they are aware of the benefits, risks, and purpose of the procedure, and give their own permission whilst in a rational mindset.

Don't worry, you don't have to know these definitions word-for-word (that's for medical school!) but having a basic understanding of these ideas and being able to apply them to scenarios, both in semi-structural interviews and MMIs, can help guide a well-thought-out answer.

The **day before your interview,** you should briefly look over your notes and feedback from your most recent practice session. Look over the answers you have planned and written out for the common general questions and memorise the main point or message that you want to get across (rather than the entire answer and exact wording). Try not to have a full practice session right before the date of your real interview, just like how it's sometimes better to avoid churning through practice papers the day before your final exam, since it often only adds to your stress levels if you come across a question you don't feel 100% prepared for. Try to rest assured that you have practised adequately and will be able to handle the majority of common questions, and if you get something uncommon, trust in your ability to think on your feet and provide an honest, insightful answer. As general advice for any upcoming assessment (no matter how many times you hear this, it's always worth repeating), go to sleep early and have a good night's rest. On the morning of your interview, have a healthy breakfast and feel free to skim over your notes if it eases your nerves.

1.6 General interview advice

The following are some overall points of advice on how to do well in the interview.

1. **Smile and introduce yourself** when you make **eye contact** with your interviewer. Offer a firm handshake and wait until you are asked to sit down or take a seat first. Once you enter the room, there will be an **implicit judgement of your demeanour,** regardless of whether it is intentional or not. Refer to the interviewers with the name they give themselves, whether it is Dr/Mr/Mrs/Ms [name], or just their first name. While the interviewer will mainly mark you on the quality of the content of your answers, you would want to make the best overall first impression of yourself as a respectful and amicable person!

2. Ensure that you are speaking with enough **volume** and that what are you saying is **clear.** Being authentic and genuinely believing in what you say will help with this, and will also hopefully aid you in conveying a passionate tone that will engage your interviewers. Don't speak too fast, nor too slow, and use professional (i.e. non-colloquial) language. Following these tips will not only help your interviewers keep up with what you are saying, hence allow a more accurate marking of the content of your answers, but also display your maturity as a potential medical student.

3. Keep your **non-verbal mannerisms** in check. In other words, **leaning forward** a little is positive body language that demonstrates you are listening to what the interviewer is saying and shows your engagement in the session. **Sit up straight** all other times and **don't slouch.** You should also **maintain eye contact** as you or the interviewer speak, and minimise any fidgety movements, such as tapping on the desk or shaking your leg. Even if you accidentally do these distracting movements, the interviewers tend to be understanding and might reassure you of the nervousness you are exhibiting.

4. Relax your nerves from the beginning, or even before the interview if possible, as it will make the rest of the interview run more smoothly. You can do this by taking **deep breaths** and doing short **mindfulness** exercises, listening to music, or talking to friends and family.

5. Talk to other candidates before your interview takes place, but only if it helps and if you are given such an opportunity. For most interviews in different universities, there is a waiting area before you are escorted by staff to the room or place where the interview occurs. It can be a great way to shake off your nerves (and their nerves too, because they are probably just as, if not more, nervous). From personal experience, I did better in the interviews where I could talk to other applicants beforehand. This was largely due to the fact that, as a consequence, I had a clearer thinking process and better articulation of my answers, all while being able to express myself and who I am as an individual.

6. Integrate your **personal experiences** into your examples, such as any volunteering you have done, extra-curricular activities, hobbies, or just things that have happened in your life that are relevant to the question. This always impresses interviewers as it adds authenticity to what you say and makes you stand out. For example, in one of my interviews, I was able to integrate the fact that I took part as a volunteer in my school's Career and Pathways Expo Night, which was relevant to the given scenario. So that not only made my answers interesting, but the volunteering aspect also demonstrated initiative and leadership. Be ready to not only talk about the situation and what happened, but to also explain your **intentions** and **actions** as well as how the experience assisted your **self-reflection** and desire to study Medicine. If it involves **conflict,** your interviewers will likely ask you about what you think was done right or wrong, and what steps you would take in future if put in similar circumstances; therefore, you should reflect on the importance of the learning process rather than just the outcome.

7. Think of the interview as a **conversation.** Think of the interviewer as just someone who wants to know more about you, which really is their role when you boil it down. Again, this assists with stress, and consequently, you can focus on authentically engaging with your interviewers.

8. Whenever you come across a term that you aren't too sure about, or if you are confused with something in a scenario, ask the interviewer for clarification! This may end up changing your entire answer, so you would save a lot of time by understanding the entire situation and giving a relevant answer from the start, compared to if you were to give an irrelevant answer and the interviewers would ask you to read the scenario and try again. Also, if you feel that you didn't completely hear the question the first time, don't be afraid to politely ask them to repeat it.

9. If you feel it is appropriate (and natural!), try to insert a few personal comments, or a joke if possible. After reading the scenario, feel free to give your first impression of what is happening, such as a comment like "this seems like quite a difficult situation and I would feel awful if I were that student." In fact, this comment shows **empathy** as well, a quality which most interviewers search for and is expected of a medical student.
10. There is **no incorrect answer** when it comes to interview questions, especially for scenarios. What the interviewer is looking for is only the depth of your thinking process, whether you have really thought through the reasons and consequences for your decision and, if there are consequences, how you accommodate for them. For ethical questions, do not be afraid to give a slightly controversial answer if that truly is what you believe in, as long as it is not completely outrageous and unethical. For example, if they ask you whether you believe in the existence of the gender pay gap, it is okay if you think it does not exist, but either way, you need to provide reasons and arguments to back up your case.
11. As a minor point of advice, do not take it to heart if you notice your interviewer constantly checking the clock as you speak. It's not them being rude; they are only trying to ensure the interview finishes on time for the next candidates! This is especially true for universities that have longer interviews that can last for around 40 to 50 minutes, hence they need to keep track of the time.
12. The best advice, however simple it may seem, is to **be yourself!** You got this interview due to your high scores, so the interviewer already knows that you are academically capable. Now, they are only looking for applicants who can meet the criteria for ideal medical students in their course – whether you are compassionate, empathetic, pragmatic, communicative, and personable. This is another reason why you should avoid memorising word-for-word answers, especially if they are from another source like what a past medical student said, since you would want everything you say to the interviewer to be authentic!

1.7 Semi-structural panel interview preparation and advice

As mentioned previously, this will involve presenting your answers in front of a panel – usually two or three interviewers – and the agenda of the interview is not as strictly timed and structured as the MMI, hence its name. You will be asked a variety of questions which can either be **general questions,** which directly assess your motivations and values, or **scenario-specific,** which gauge different qualities in a less direct sense. For example, a general question may ask you to "describe a time when you have worked out a conflict that arose. Tell us how you dealt with this conflict." and a scenario-specific question may ask "if you were an employer, how would you deal with a conflict between two employees where one was passed over for a promotion in favour of the other?" Both look for your problem-solving and teamwork skills, and potentially empathy, but the manner in which these are judged differ greatly.

One of the first steps you should take, when you know the university will be holding a semi-structural interview, is to research the university and its course itself. A highly common question is "Why do you want to study here?", and reasons as to why you want to study Medicine are not enough. The interviewers want to know why you are applying for their particular course, as opposed to other universities, which directly implies that you need to note the key features which make their course unique and stand out. In addition, researching the university also gives you a great opportunity to ask any questions about the curriculum, or scientific research conducted by the university. The best time to add this in is **at the end of the interview,** where your interviewers will ask you if you have any questions or if you want to add to any of your answers. Whilst these questions are not mandatory or essential for their marking, it certainly leaves a good impression in the panel's mind about your level of enthusiasm for entering their course, which may mean a higher score if they are marking holistically.

As a general point of polite behaviour, and something that is often neglected, at the end you should **thank your interviewers** for their time. They usually have quite busy schedules, especially if they introduce themselves to you as doctors, so showing your appreciation displays your professionalism and leaves a lasting impression as you walk out the door.

When it is time for a scenario, you will most likely be given a laminated piece of paper with the scenario on it right in front of you. Your interviewer will read it out loud first then start asking you the related questions. Don't panic if you find yourself not being able to give an answer straight after the panel asks the question. In fact, it is better to ask them for a minute so that you can read over the scenario again since this increases the likelihood of giving a stronger yet concise answer, rather than waffling and not reaching a clear-cut answer.

Preparing for interviews can be difficult for many people as there is a huge variety in the advice you may receive. Some may tell you that you can get away with virtually no preparation as the assessors dislike rehearsed answers, while others may insist that the only way to succeed is through careful memorisation of responses. Many people have attained places in medical school through both of these methods, but in my experience, the way to give yourself the highest chance of success is to **take the middle road!** You want to prepare enough that you won't be thrown off by an unexpected question, yet you don't want to sacrifice the impressive flair that comes with an off-the-cuff answer. It may be difficult to achieve this perfect balance, but the right type and amount of preparation can put you in an ideal position.

A good first step to take when preparing for the interview is to think about **what you have done in your life.** Of course, the interviewers are aware that you are probably a recent high school graduate, so the expectations aren't particularly high, however a surprising number of questions are usually about your past. Try to focus on things you have done that are non-academic such as volunteering, sporting, or music achievements. The interviewers will assume you have the academic strength to be good enough to enter their medical degree and are looking for other qualities and interests in your life that demonstrate you are a balanced individual. One of the common interview questions that ties into this idea goes something along the lines of "what are you most proud of achieving?" When answering this, you want to avoid falling into the trap of boasting about an academic achievement. Showing humility in this situation is difficult, but if you mention a non-academic achievement you are genuinely proud of, the interviewers will likely be more impressed. If you are struggling to think of anything, then you could go with something more generic such as being proud of working hard during your GCSEs/A-Levels, although this is still related to academic achievement and thus not ideal.

Once you have had a think about the things you have done so far, it is time to build up a **memory bank of valuable experiences** you have had in your life. You can consider these as **personal anecdotes for you to inject into your answers** to give them a boost when you are asked about something that's happened in your life. The worst-case scenario in an interview for you to be left scratching your head when asked a tough question like "tell us about a time when you had to resolve conflict." There's nothing wrong with taking a pause to consider how to structure your answer, but spending 30 seconds 'um'ing and 'ah'ing is quite unpleasant. Having a selection of meaningful life events in your memory makes this situation much less likely, as you will have already given thought to how these can be applied to demonstrate a particular value or quality you have. I would suggest you have a think about some anecdotes so you have at least one for each of the following topics:
- Teamwork
- Leadership
- Empathy
- Decision making
- Communication skills
- Commitment to improvement
- Conflict resolution
- Cultural sensitivity

1.7 Semi-structural panel interview preparation and advice

These are all important skills for doctors to have, so it is likely you will be asked to discuss moments in your life where you demonstrated these attributes. Obviously, you can add to this list if you feel you have an excellent anecdote that doesn't fit into one of these categories. Once you have spent time thinking about and memorising your anecdotes, you should start applying them to practice questions. On page 96, there is a list of common interview questions which is a great place to start. You should see how easily you can adapt your anecdotes to suit each question. If you find yourself struggling, you should spend some more time thinking about the question and maybe add to your list of anecdotes.

One of the key aspects of answering interview questions is having **depth** to your responses. This not only comes from adding your personal experiences, but also having a **robust structure.** Instead of rehearsing answers for each of these questions, you should keep a solid structure in mind. This means you will have some prepared content to fall back on in case an unexpected question is asked, while giving yourself an opportunity to answer it honestly and in a genuine manner. Remember, the interviewers will be looking out for rehearsed answers, so don't go into any specific details with your planned structures, just have some ideas or themes you want to explore in conjunction with your personal anecdotes to give a well-rounded response.

When you feel ready, you should have a family member or friend test you by asking an assortment of randomly selected questions from the list. Saying your answers out loud to another person is the best way to simulate the interview conditions. The mock interviewer should be able to give feedback about the content of your response, along with other areas for improvement. It is often the **non-verbal aspects** of your responses that influence the interviewers the most. You should always present yourself as a **confident** and **professional** individual, maintaining enough eye contact with all interviewers and sitting in an open and friendly manner. There are many non-verbal cues that influence people, so you might be surprised by the feedback you receive. It may also be helpful to have someone film some of your answers. While analysing yourself on a recording can be an uncomfortable experience, it provides valuable insight into what steps you need to take to improve your overall presentation and technique.

One of the key things you must do as part of your interview preparation is to **research the university you are applying for.** You should see if the university has published any information about the interview on their website. For instance, you can find information about the general topics assessed by the semi-structural interview on the relevant university's websites, which you can use to guide your preparation. Along with this, it is equally important to research the university course itself. A common interview question is, "why do you want to study at our university?" so you should explore what aspects of that degree really set it apart from other courses. You should be able to find a few things to discuss through a simple internet search, but try to also talk to students who are currently studying at the institution if you know any.

1.8 MMI preparation and advice

Typically as a domestic student, you will have 8 active stations and one rest station, all arranged in a 'circuit.' In an active station, you have 10 minutes total, 2 minutes to read the scenario (which is often pasted on the door of your interview room) and 8 minutes to answer the interviewer's questions. In a rest station, you have 10 minutes to simply sit down quietly and relax.

For each active station, you will be given one scenario and five questions related to it. With you, there will be eight other applicants, as you all rotate around each station in the circuit, and an accompanying staff member who will supervise your group. Often, the staff member will ring a bell to indicate that time is up and that you should move on to your next station. After your first station, you will have 2 minutes to move to the next station and read the scenario while the interviewers finalise their scoring and prepare for the next candidate. In total, a 'circuit' will take around 90 to 100 minutes to finish. After your interview as a whole has completed, you may be sequestered and taken as a group to a separate place to wait, giving time for interviewers to finalise their marking and for the faculty to arrange the next set of applicants for the next time slot. This sequestering may only take a few minutes to ensure one group of candidates do not interact with the next (i.e. to prevent candidates discussing scenarios or questions), or it may last for a few hours, depending on the university's schedule. For example, interviewees for 2018 entry in a certain university had to be sequestered for around three hours so that the faculty could conduct research regarding the Situational Judgement Test (SJT), where the applicants took the computer test and then were able to leave as a large group.

Get an idea of the attributes that a university's interview will be focused on looking for, mainly by looking at their website on the **Admissions Requirements** or **How to Apply** pages for their medical program. The most common attributes that interviewers evaluate are:

- Advocacy
- Empathy
- Collaboration
- Critical thinking
- Motivation
- Ethical reasoning

Since the assessment of these traits is integrated within the scenarios of each of the stations, there is no easy way of predicting the kind of situations you will be faced with, thus it becomes harder to prepare answers beforehand. However, something that you can do is that you can brainstorm based off these listed abstract concepts, starting with examples of how you demonstrated a particular trait. For example, you may have exhibited collaboration and critical thinking when dealing with a complex conflict between team members for a group project at school, and helped to come up with a solution that eased tensions on both sides. Via volunteering experiences, such as at a hospital or with an ambulance service, you could have also demonstrated advocacy and empathy. It all depends on the specific setting that an experience occurred, where you can focus on some aspects more than others to emphasise certain attributes.

Finally, do not worry if you think you completely flunked one or two stations. The final interview score you will achieve depends on your overall performance in all of the stations, rather than just individual stations. This means that you can compensate for a station you had little confidence in with a station that you felt you went really well in. The most important thing, if you do feel like you mess up a bit, is to move on and do your utmost to perform better in the stations that come after.

1.9 Answer structures

In general, a good interview response question will be shaped like a **barrel:** narrow at the top and bottom, but wide in the middle. In other words, you should start and end your answer with a clear and concise point, then use the middle of your answer to flesh out your thought processes and bring up relevant anecdotes or ideas. For example, compare the following two potential responses:

Question: Have you ever had to compromise something important to you?	
Response 1: "I really try hard not to compromise on the things that are truly important to me because my values like honesty and integrity and really important to me and I don't believe they should be compromised. But a time where I've had to do this has been in my GCSEs where I have had to compromise some of my interpersonal relationships with friends in order to dedicate myself to my studies. My friends are extremely important to me, but doing well in exams is essential for my future, so I've had to compromise my closeness with them to spend more time studying. An example of this would have been the week where my two best friends had their 16th birthdays in one week, but I had three big assessment tasks due, so I had to tell them I could only stay for a little while."	**Response 2:** "Yes, I have. I'm typically a person my friends know they can come to when they're feeling upset, and I'm grateful that they trust me in that capacity. But I recall one day during the GCSE exam period when a friend called me after school in tears about how her exam that day had gone. I was extremely stressed because I had three exams back-to-back the next day, and I was also not feeling confident about the exam we had sat that afternoon, so I was incredibly dismissive and just told her to get over it and focus on the next exams because that's what I was doing. In hindsight, I would have tried to be much more gentle and patient, but my other commitments meant I had to compromise my role as the compassionate friend in order to look after myself. I spoke to her about it afterwards and apologised for being brusque, but that moment taught me I need to be aware of my own breaking points so that I don't have to make such sudden compromises that can affect other people. I like to think I'm much better at managing this now, and communicating to others when I need to make compromises."

Notice how the first response seems to meander between different talking points without much direction? It starts with a vague, personal philosophy about compromise, then goes on to describe a fairly generic scenario before providing a specific example right at the end. The fact that the answer ends with evidence leaves no room for self-reflection or an overall conclusion to the response, so the whole thing feels ill-thought-out. By contrast, the second response begins with a straightforward "yes" – while it seems obvious, beginning with something simple like this can 'ease' the interviewers into the rest of your answer, and also introduces them to the general direction that your response will take. Another thing the second response does well is that it **begins simply, then gets more detailed.** The answer elaborates on the experience and sets the scene so that assessors can logically follow your train of thought. Finally, after characterising the circumstances and explaining how this was an example of a compromise, the second response shifts to focus on the lessons learned from this experience, and concludes with an optimistic note about approaching similar situations in the future.

One great strategy to help with structuring how you should relay any personal experiences is to follow the acronym **STARR** (Situation, Task, Actions, Results, Reflection).

- **Situation:** this is where you give a short description of the setting (i.e. who, when, where, if relevant).
- **Task:** this is where you say what you had to do and what problems you encountered.
- **Actions:** this refers to the steps you took to tackle any issues you came across (which gives you an opportunity to show your initiative).
- **Results:** this means what happened due to your actions – was the problem solved, or did things get worse?
- **Reflection:** this is when you say what you learnt from the situation, what you did that did not go so well, and what you should do in similar circumstances in the future (which makes this the most important component of your answer).

Ensuring that there is some sort of a structure to what you say adds to your coherence, allowing the interviewers to better follow what you say, and is sure to boost your score.

One more important piece of advice is to **never sit on the fence,** whether it be in answering questions or responding to scenarios. For example, if you were asked a question like "do you prefer working in a team or by yourself?" you may be tempted to say that you have no preference and can adapt to any situation, thus making yourself sound as good as possible to the interviewers... but consistently using this kind of response can come across as disingenuous, or can indicate a lack of self-reflection and assertiveness.

In this example, there is *nothing* wrong with preferring teamwork or working by yourself. As long as you articulate your answer well and explore multiple facets of the question, your final answer will not reflect poorly on you. This is especially true when you are faced with a tough decision in a scenario question. In the end, the interviewers don't really care what your answer is, as long as you've considered both sides of the issue and demonstrated qualities such as critical thinking and empathy.

And the final piece of advice is for you to view this as a **learning experience!** Even if this isn't the first interview of your life, it certainly won't be the last, so try to take on board all the advice you receive as you never know when you might need it. There is no doubt you will feel very nervous going into the interview, but remember that this is but one opportunity to get into Medicine, and that there will always be new paths you can take to reach your goals. At the end of the day, you can only give it your best shot!

1.10 Sample interview questions

> **SAMPLE :**
> *You have recently been hired to run a charity that is dedicated to preserving the critically endangered yellowhammer. This species of bird is found across the UK but is shrinking in population due to degradation of its natural habitat and the reduction in its food availability due to pesticide use. Outline what steps you would take to ensure the survival of the yellowhammer and allow this species to thrive.*

This scenario is somewhat unconventional as there are no moral or ethical dilemmas involved, however the structure and content of your answer is extremely important. Skills associated with **critical thinking, succinct reasoning, efficient communication** and **decision making** are all going to be assessed by the interviewers when listening to your answer, so it is vital to spend some time thinking about your response before you start speaking. The scenario gives you a fair bit of scope to explore many aspects of running the hypothetical charity using your general knowledge. The best way to approach this problem is to discuss how to increase funding for your charity and then outline your plan for allocating this money in a way that would allow for the yellowhammer to thrive.

In terms of securing funding, the most appropriate channels for this scenario would be government assistance and donations. You could suggest meeting with representatives from the environmental division of the government to see if your charity could be allocated money as part of the official response to rehabilitate the species. This could also involve working with zoos and other wildlife reserves to reinforce the relationship. In order to increase donations, you need to raise awareness about the issue, particularly in areas where the bird is a cherished part of the ecosystem. Affordable methods include hosting events, purchasing billboards, launching social media campaigns, or running local radio advertisements. You should also consider investment in recruiting volunteers, as they are essential to ensure that all events run smoothly and are cost efficient.

Now that you have discussed a number of potentially avenues to financially sustain the charity, you need to address how you would ensure the survival of the yellowhammer. The interviewers do not expect you to have any specific knowledge about the yellowhammer or action plans to save endangered species, so don't concern yourself with the details. They are looking for a practical plan that shows you can make reliable decisions when given a short amount of time. Communication is also very important for this scenario, and arguably the way you present your plan is more important than the content. In terms of actually responding to the scenario, the most logical course of action would be to prevent degradation of their food supply and pesticide use, which is mentioned in the prompt as the reason for their decline in population. This could involve negotiating with official services to protect areas of natural habitat and sending volunteers to rehabilitate native wildlife and restore the ecosystem. Introduced predators and diseases also tend to be threats to native animals, so researching methods to control these would be beneficial for the yellowhammer population. Another excellent idea would be to start a captive breeding program in conjunction with a zoo or wildlife reserve. You may have already mentioned a partnership of some kind with these entities, so starting a program like this would be a natural step to take and would ensure the survival of the species. Of course, this is quite a bit more specialised than the previous suggestions, so don't be worried if your general knowledge on the subject does not extend that far.

> **SAMPLE:**
> *You are a third year medical student preparing for your end of year examinations, which are coming up in a week's time. Your grandfather who lives in the same city has recently become ill, and requires constant care. You have no family members who are available to help this week. Explain your actions in this scenario.*

This scenario raises the issue of prioritisation and how to balance the stress of work with the obligations you have in your life. It is very clear that both obligations are very serious as your grandfather requires constant care, yet you need lots of time to study so you can pass your exams. This scenario is important as you may be put in a similar position throughout medical school and also in your career as a doctor, so you to have a way to deal with this, especially if you cannot rely on your family.

With all scenario questions, you should first establish unknowns and knowns. To demonstrate empathy towards your grandfather, you should look for ways to care for him without sacrificing your study. We are told that there are no family members around to help you, but there might be friends or neighbours. Asking if you have friends to assist you is usually a good way to start, though in this scenario they will most likely be also studying for exams, so it is unfair to look to them for help at this time. The interviewer will likely affirm this point, so it would be time to look for more professional help in this situation. You should explore the possibility of hiring a nurse or carer for the duration of the week, arranging a schedule for neighbours to check up on your grandfather and help out where they can, and even checking to see if he is sick enough to be admitted into a hospital, given he may require this constant care beyond just the time it takes him to recover from his illness.

Finding a pragmatic solution that ensures your grandfather's health and safety is secured whilst you have adequate time to prepare for your exams is the goal here, but you would need to be reasonable in your approach. For instance, your answer could perhaps mention finding the most efficient ways to study, and making alternate arrangements for any other commitments you have to ensure these two important priorities are met. Ultimately, the interviewers will force you into making a decision, but this scenario is not really about choosing between your grandfather and studies. The interviewers want to know if **you can ask for help in difficult situations when you are out of your depth.** For instance, a great response would mention seeking advice from mentors or university staff. You could also request a different examination schedule which would allow you more time to study, or if this is not possible, you could notify the relevant staff about your current situation, and they may be able to grant you special considerations because of your difficult circumstances.

In your career as a doctor, there will be many times where you will not be able to safely undertake a task on your own. You need to be able to recognise this, and ask the appropriate person to assist you. This doesn't just apply to issues with work, but also emotional and social problems that are causing you undue stress. In this case, you should bring up the option of discussing your problem with someone who is senior in the medical school administration. It may not seem like it, given the intense workloads, but medical schools are trying to be more supportive to their students, particularly given the mental health issues that are becoming apparent amongst medical students and doctors. Accordingly, you should also be conscious of your mental health while preparing for the UCAT, your interviews, or any assessment task, and never be afraid to ask for help when needed!

Best of luck for the UCAT exam and with your journey to Medicine!